Ireland explored

an illustrated travel guide

BRANDON

For Ciarán

Text, illustrations and book design by Ditty Kummer
With the assistance (text) of Ciarán O'Connor
Edited by Siobhán Parkinson
Typed by Lorna Kennedy
Typesetting and colour separation by IGS, Rotterdam, The Netherlands
Printing and binding by Brepols, Turnhout, Belgium

British Library Cataloguing
in Publication Data

Kummer, Ditty
Ireland explored: an illustrated travel guide.
1. Ireland – Description and travel – 1981 – Guide-books.
I. Title
914.15'04824 DA980
ISBN 0-86322-082-7

First published 1986
Brandon Book Publishers Ltd,
Dingle, Co. Kerry;

Ireland explored

an illustrated travel guide

Ditty Kummer

The cover illustration shows the valley near Laragh in County Wicklow.
Previous page shows Newtown Castle near Ballyvaghan, County Clare.
These pages show Killykeen Forest Park near Cavan.

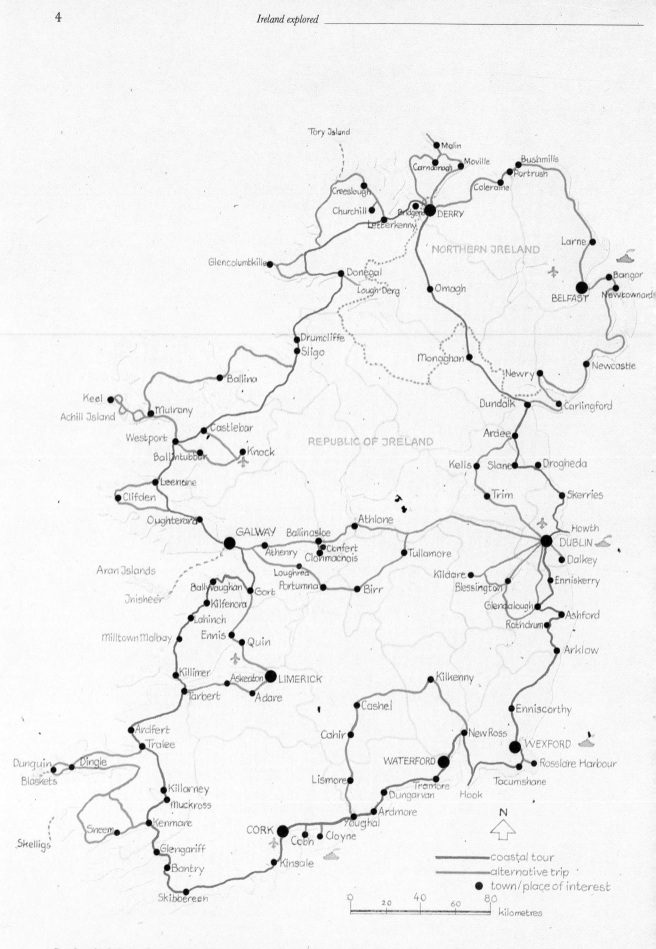

How to use this guide

The tour around Ireland follows a logical coastal route covering the most interesting and beautiful locations. There are also some alternative trips which give a selection of other places of special interest. Depending on your personal preferences and the time you have available, you can adapt and interlink sections of the described routes. As a rough guide, you would need about four weeks to complete the whole coastal trip, with perhaps an extra week if you want to take in some of the alternatives.

Ireland is best explored by car, particularly if you wish to visit the more remote places. Public transport is reasonable in Dublin and between the main towns and cities, but in country areas the service is poor. Hitch-hiking is safer in Ireland than elsewhere in Europe and offers an opportunity to meet the Irish, who seem to prefer to lift foreigners than fellow-citizens. Friendly curiosity is an Irish attribute you will meet more than once.

In places like Dingle and Connemara a bicycle is an excellent way to experience the landscape and monuments that abound in such beautiful harmony.

At the end of each chapter you will find an accurate and detailed map, accompanied by precise route descriptions. These maps correspond to four holiday maps printed by the Ordnance Survey, called 'Ireland North, East, South and West'. They are valuable and informative general maps and are the only other essential material you will need on your tour. If you want all four maps bound in book form, then buy the _Ordnance Survey – Road Atlas of Ireland,_ published by Gill & Macmillan. But if by chance you do get lost because there are no signposts or because you misread maps, remember the Irish saying 'When God made time he made plenty of it.'

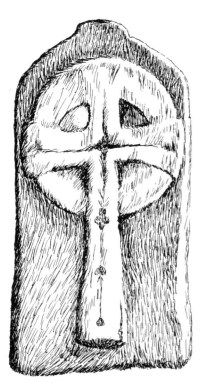

Cross slab in Latin form near St Kevin's church, Glendalough, County Wicklow

Introduction

Ireland is the only nation with predominantly Celtic roots. In written form the Irish language (Gaelic) is the third oldest European language after Greek and Latin. The earliest writings by Christian monks record an even older oral tradition of epic heroic literature, 'The joint memory of ancients, the transmission from one ear to another, the chanting of the poets.'

The early Christian missionaries to Ireland in the fifth century found here a highly organised society with specialists in customary law, heroic literature, genealogy and the sacred arts. They supplanted paganism and the druids with Christianity and religious schools of learning, but altered little else. The existing artistic skills of the people were put to use, and Celtic motifs were incorporated into beautiful manuscripts such as the Book of Kells and the gold, silver and stone work inspired by the new faith. A rich Christian-Celtic culture existed until the final defeat of Irish chieftains in 1601 at the Battle of Kinsale by English forces.

The native Irish culture declined until the 'Celtic Twilight' revival of the late nineteenth and early twentieth centuries initiated mainly by the poet W. B. Yeats. This cultural reawakening mirrored a renewed political awareness, and an armed struggle finally achieved independence for the southern part of Ireland in 1921.

Today Ireland has the youngest population in Europe and faces serious social and economic problems. However, it is still special for its music, literature and outlook on life as well as its physical beauty.

The aim of this book is to paint a socio-cultural portrait of Ireland and to provide a practical tour guide to the country. It is based on my own travels around this lovely land. I have tried to capture the features and atmosphere of the chosen places in the drawings, watercolours and linocuts I have selected.

I hope you will enjoy your trips(s) as much as I did and that this book will be a memento of your visit after the taste of Guinness and the sound of the *uileann* pipes have faded.

Or do Mhíchíl: 'A prayer for Michael', cross slab in Clonmacnois, county Offaly

Contents

Chapter 1

County Wicklow

Wicklow is called the garden of Ireland and it combines very beautiful green scenery with countless places of interest. If you stay in or around Dublin, you will probably make a few trips to this garden, so I have suggested three alternative routes, which also can be combined with the coastal tour around Ireland.

The Wicklow mountains are mainly of granite and contain such minerals as zinc and copper, so there are mines, especially in the valley near Avoca. One side of a mountain might appear completely intact, while the other side has been gouged out by open-cast mining. Many mines have been closed now and present a sad spectacle of abused and bare hills. Their fate is to be turned into dumping places...

Central Wicklow is wooded and mountainous, penetrated by deep glens, lakes, rivers and waterfalls. This rough country is crossed by a military road fifty kilometres long, which runs from Rathfarnham – just south of Dublin – to Aghavannagh. The road was built after the 1798 rising* to make the mountains more accessible to the British army. Like a ribbon thrown over the mountaintops it offers today's travellers the most gorgeous views. I recommend a trip via the military road very warmly! But if you have not much time at least visit Powerscourt Gardens near Enniskerrry and Glendalough monastic site near Laragh. These two places are an absolute must.

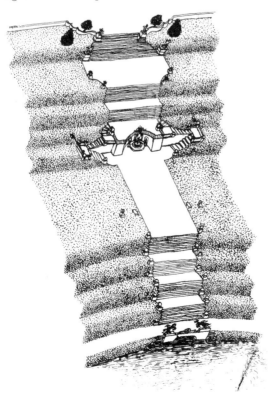

A bird's eye view of the steps of Powerscourt Gardens near Enniskerry

---

*This was an armed rebellion by Irish nationalists against the English (see page 25).

Powerscourt Gardens, Enniskerry

You may take the main road from Dublin to Enniskerry, but my suggested route gives the real flavour of Wicklow (see page 23). This way you will drive via Stepaside, which immediately presents you with the first of the Wicklow glens near the Scalp, and, as you drive, gives you many changing perpectives of the Great Sugarloaf mountain, an important feature of the Powerscourt Gardens themselves.

Unfortunately Powerscourt House was destroyed by fire in 1976,

This gateway leads to the former 'City of Glendalough', which is described on the next pages. The gate is the only surviving example of its kind in Ireland.

but the walls of main building remain standing and the adjacent buildings are still intact. It ought to be restored or at least preserved for even in its present state it looks magnificent.

The symmetrical Victorian terraced garden is very extensive. The fine decorated steps form a strong central axis between the house and the natural environment. When you descend them you feel as if you are stepping into a huge bowl, covered with green velvet. It is a delight to walk the curved grass terraces and to see the volcano-shaped Great Sugarloaf change from a distant hill to an impressive mountain again. At the bottom of the bowl lies a circular mirror, the

In Glendalough lived an old saint,

Renowned for his learning and piety,

His good manners he wouldn't taint,

to be mixed up with female society.

Opposite page: Impression of the solemn round tower, the watchpost of Glenda lough

pool gleaming mysteriously with its own secret life beneath the surface, like *Tír na nÓg* (the Land of Youth) of Irish fairy tales. In the sun the water of the fountain in the centre of the pool looks like silver wire, tied up to the vault of heaven.

On the lower terrace to the left is a so-called Japanese garden, which has fallen into decay. There is a real Japanese garden in Kildare, which is described on page 23.

Powerscourt Waterfall nearby is a favourite picnic place for many Dubliners. A typical Sunday sees the family arriving between two and three p.m. parking as close to the river as safety allows and listening to the radio or reading the Sunday paper. Around five p.m. they will pack their deck-chairs, radio and paper, yet they will probably leave their rubbish behind.

Now drive on to Laragh and Glendalough, through another part of the splendid Wicklow landscape. When you look to your left you'll see Djouce mountain, which is part of the Wicklow Way, a nature walk which starts in Rathfarnham, county Dublin, and leads to the southern counties of Ireland.

Glendalough monastic site

First of all I must offer my apologies for using too many superlatives in the following description of Glendalough monastic site, but it was love at the first sight, you see. Undoubtedly the former monastic

One of the Celtic crosses with a background of yews in moonlit Glendalough

settlement of Clonmacnois in county Offaly is architecturally more interesting, but it can't be compared with the special atmosphere of my favourite site.

Glendalough, the Glen of the Two Lakes, is lovely in both rain and sunshine. The rain falls frequently in this valley, but it is striking to watch the heavy clouds moving over the glen. While they are emptying their wet cargo on this holy place, they make trees dark green and soft grass glossy and fragrant.

The sun disappears behind the solemn round tower, leaving fiery beams around its outline, so that it looks just as it must have done in former times when set on fire by plunderers.

In the evening sun the grave-stones have long, deformed shadows, and from a distance their shady sides form a splendid black silhouette against the pale green slope of the glen.

Glendalough, also called the City of the Seven Churches, was built by Saint Kevin in the sixth century. He is said to be Ireland's second most famous saint – after Saint Patrick of course! You will find Kevin's cell, Kevin's bed, Kevin's cross and Kevin's church here too. The latter is also called Kevin's kitchen, altough he only used to sleep here. This building has a fine high-pitched roof in corbel style, which means that each layer of loose stones overlaps the other until they meet at the top. The small round tower at one end matches its nearby bigger brother perfectly.

In many legends, songs and poems about Glendalough** the holy father Kevin is the central character. I like the story about his meeting with Kathleen-of-the-eyes-of-most-unholy-blue. She tried to seduce him, although he was bound by holy vows. To slow her advances he beat her with a bunch of nettles! There is also a poem mentioning another effort to cool her passion. It says that he 'threw her into the black lake shrieking'. Whether it is true or not, it makes the history of Glendalough more lively. Another old tradition claims that seven visits to this place are equal to a pilgrimage to Rome, but only if you have a special dispensation... I wonder if frequent visitors such as myself might qualify for this exemption?

Mount Usher Gardens, Ashford

If you have seen enough of Glendalough – you can't really have enough of it – and feel like travelling on, Mount Usher Gardens in Ashford might please you. These gardens have been described very positively in many guides and booklets. Their recommendations sounded convincing and since Ashford is close to Glendalough I thought it worth a visit. But Mount Usher did not live up to my expectations....

The gardens are designed in the Romantic style of the late nineteenth century. That works well in the areas planted with trees, where beautiful species of pines are specially worth a closer look. You can choose different tree-walks, but only the palm-walk has the coherence which I would like to see in the other parts of the garden. The Romantic 'natural' style really depends on a hidden structure to work effectively but in Mount Usher some areas are too closely planted, possibly because of changes in ownership and lack of

Opposite page: Mount Usher Gardens near Ashford: a view of the lovely water and to the left the beginning of the lime-walk

**There is a new 'interpretive centre' which provides lots of information and guided tours.

maintenance. This creates a fussy image in contrast to a designed effect.

The water, however, is lovely. The river Vartry flows over many weirs, under bailey-bridges and through ponds and wells.

Except for the house, which might formerly have been a porter's lodge, the jumble of buildings at the entrance is very ugly and does not complement the gardens at all.

Meet you in 'The Meetings'

Avondale Forest Park, an excellent place for walking and cycling, is adjacent to Rathdrum, a small village with genuine country pubs. Further on is the Meeting of the Waters, where the rivers Avonmore and Avonbeg meet. A pub, appropriately named 'The Meetings' marks – you might say mars – the spot, but you should not judge Irish pubs by their appearance, because the nicest ones sometimes look very ugly. 'The Meetings' has a huge glassy ballroom glued to the back wall, from where you have a view of the two little rivers, but in spite of this clumsy addition the place has a good atmosphere and people, young and old, do meet here. On a Sunday afternoon whole families are united, grannies, toddlers and babies in prams included. Women exchange the local gossip, enjoying a Martini or a short (strong alcoholic drink with a dash of lemonade). Men do men's things like playing cards or darts and if the 'crack' (witty talk) is as good and as flowing as the Guinness then it will, by all accounts, be a

The front of this house in Rathdrum tells a story about its inhabitants. They are still skilled in the valuable Irish tradition of handpainted lettering. They take care of the appearance of the premises by repairing cracks in the plasterwork, before repainting the wall. The colours chosen are warm and express a popular approach to colour, with a preference for very bright tones, which in most cases works well. P(addy?) Cullen is shop-owner, barman and undertaker, the latter appropriately connected with the gate...

The polluted area around the NET works near Woodenbridge

grand day.... Children have fun together, eating ice-cream, sweets, crisps or all three at once.

One night I went to 'The Meetings' to listen to the Fureys, a band which plays a kind of traditional gypsy music. The group has a certain reputation, so the place is packed. Teenagers reassure each other in noisy groups and walk up and down continuously, as much to be seen as to see. Elderly people patiently wait for the music to

The eclectic entrance lodge to the picnic place near Woodenbridge, built in 1888

begin and when it does the tables are crowded with bottles and glasses.

The climax is reached when the band plays 'Sweet Sixteen', a pretty, sentimental song and everybody sings along. We want to hear more, but the event ends punctually at half eleven with everyone who can stand on their feet singing the national anthem. Once the pints are finished all go home satisfied, although outside I hear people commenting on the big fee the group were paid for 'only one and a half hours!'

Woodenbridge

The road from Avoca, near 'The Meetings' leads to Woodenbridge and a pleasant picnic site in a forest lay-by. When you climb the narrow paths you get a view of a bright green golf-course in the distance and many rhododendrons to the forefront. Continuing to Arklow the greenery begins to fade and eventually disappears. The cause is a state fertiliser project, NET, whose dirty yellowish fall-out has killed every blade of grass in the nearby area. I can only hope that, in its bid to industrialise and give employment to its people, Ireland does not make the mistake of developing similar polluting industries.

Now you will cross the border to county Wexford which is described in the next chapter.

Alternative routes

Russborough House, Blessington

From the centre of Dublin you can drive directly to Blessington and from there on signposts help you to find Russborough, a fine Georgian house built around 1740. The scenery is not particularly remarkable, but I love the tall beeches which were planted by the original owner.

The house is sober and symmetrical outside but very richly furnished inside, containing Irish silver and the famous Beit collection of paintings. Every room has a beautiful plasterwork ceiling, the one in the music room is acoustically shaped and covered with flower motifs enlarging near its edges.

In the rich plasterwork over the stairs is a big crescent moon

The almost austere features of Russborough near Blessington, the longest Georgian house in Ireland

Entrance to a former forge in Aughrim in the style of the 1850s. The dressing around the door is in cut granite.

with a laughing face, said to be an accurate caricature of the first owner of the house. The wily plasterer was of course an Irishman and although his work at the time was considered 'the ravings of a maniac', he has had the last laugh…

Glen of Imaal & Glenmalure

You get a superb impression of Wicklow's beauty when you continue from Blessington up to the south side of the Glen of Imaal. In Derrynamuck is Dwyer's cottage, where Michael

Glen of Imaal. Unfortunately this area is partly occupied by the army. Warning signs were posted after children had picked up an unexploded shell, with fatal consequences.

Dwyer, leader of the famous Wicklow resistance in the 1798 rising (see page 25) was trapped by the English. You can have a look inside if you like.

Red signs warn that some areas are dangerous because of military exercises. But if you stay on the road you safely reach Laragh, through the rugged valley of Glenmalure. From here the Military Road continues to Sally Gap. The river Glenmacnass is on your left as the road leads straight uphill. At the top is the Glenmacnass Waterfall, also a visual high point, with extremely clear water streaming over flat smooth stones. Below is the valley, nicely dotted with bushes and firmly held together by two

rugged glens. In the far distance are more mountains, hidden in a veil of soft mist.

If you turn back to Dublin, you will have, on a calm evening, a lovely view of the city below, mysterious with twinkling lights everywhere.

Japanese Gardens, Kildare

A trip to the Japanese Gardens in Kildare can be linked with the visit to Russborough, but it is also a pleasant start if you want to

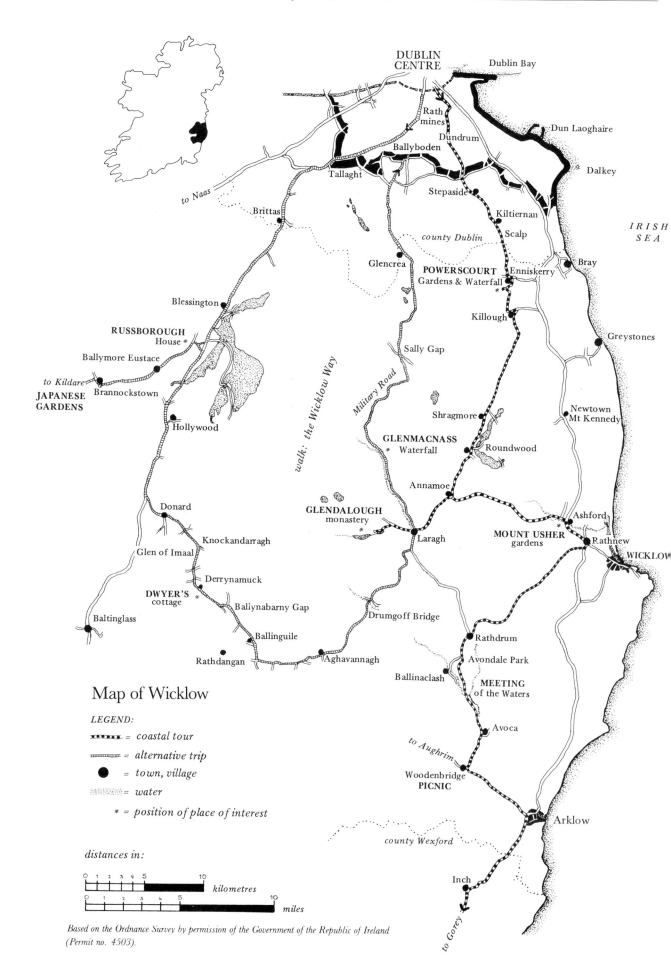

DUBLIN CENTRE

Dublin Bay

Rath mines

Dundrum

Dun Laoghaire

Ballyboden

Dalkey

Tallaght

Stepaside

Kiltiernan

IRISH SEA

Scalp

Brittas

county Dublin

Glencrea

POWERSCOURT
Gardens & Waterfall

Enniskerry

Bray

Blessington

Killough

RUSSBOROUGH
House *

Greystones

Ballymore Eustace

Sally Gap

to Kildare
JAPANESE
GARDENS

Brannockstown

Shragmore

Newtown
Mt Kennedy

Hollywood

GLENMACNASS
*   Waterfall

Roundwood

Donard

Annamoe

Ashford

GLENDALOUGH
monastery
*

MOUNT USHER
gardens

Rathnew

Knockandarragh

Laragh

WICKLOW

Glen of Imaal

Derrynamuck

DWYER'S
cottage   *

Ballynabarny Gap

Drumgoff Bridge

Baltinglass

Ballinguile

Rathdrum

Rathdangan

Aghavannagh

Avondale Park

Ballinaclash

MEETING
of the Waters

Map of Wicklow

LEGEND:

= coastal tour

= alternative trip

● = town, village

= water

* = position of place of interest

to Aughrim

Avoca

Woodenbridge
PICNIC

Arklow

distances in:

county Wexford

0 1 2 3 4 5   10
kilometres

0 1   2   3   4   5   10
miles

Inch

to Gorey

go right across the country and visit Kerry or Clare. The gardens are near the National Stud and are signposted, but not very clearly. However, you will get there eventually.

An Irish lord gave a commission to two Japanese designers in 1906 to lay out a garden which would symbolise The Life Of Man, from the cradle to the grave.

The 'path of adventure' is very special, leading the adolescent step by step over flagstones, first surrounded by earth, later by water. At the end there is a choice of three paths – the carefree life, bachelorhood or wedded life. Of course 'man' chooses the latter, which turns out to be a reasonably happy mariage.

Standing on the 'hill of ambition' you have an overall view of this miniature life of man with its joy, obstructions and failures. I find it amazing how the designers managed to find symbols for almost every possible happening in life. You hardly need an explanation, although every visitor is given an explanatory leaflet. At the end of our lives in this garden we all pass on… We cross the red bridge of life where our souls and mortal selves pass the gateway to eternity, with an opportunity to spend our earthly riches on Japanese dwarf-trees in the nursery centre.

Coastal tour Wicklow

Route descriptions correspond with map on opposite page.

Route to Powerscourt
Dublin centre – Rathmines – Dundrum (R117) – Stepaside – Kiltiernan/Scalp – Enniskerry: Powerscourt Gardens and Waterfall.

Route to Glendalough
Continue from Enniskerry – Killough (R755) – Shragmore – Roundwood – Annamoe – Laragh (R756): Glendalough.

Route to Mount Usher Gardens and county Wexford
From Glendalough back to Annamoe (R755) – Ashford (R763): Mount Usher Gardens. To Wexford: Ashford(N11) – Rathnew – Rathdrum (R752) – the Meeting of the Waters – Avoca – Woodenbridge: Picnic place – Arklow – county Wexford.

Alternative trips

Russborough, Blessington
Dublin centre (N81) – Tallaght – Brittas – Blessington: Russborough House.

Glen of Imaal, Glenmalure
Continue from Russborough House to Hollywood – Donard – Knockandarragh – Derrynamuck: Dwyer's Cottage – Ballinabarny Gap – Ballinguile – Aghavannagh (Military Road) – Drumgoff Bridge – Laragh – Glenmacnass Waterfall – Sally Gap (R115) – Glencrea – Ballyboden – Dublin.

Kildare – Japanese Gardens
Continue from Russborough (see alternative 1) to Ballymore Eustace – Brannockstown (R413) – Kilcullen – Kildare: Japanese Gardens and National Stud.

From Kildare road N7 leads directly to the counties Limerick, Clare or Kerry.

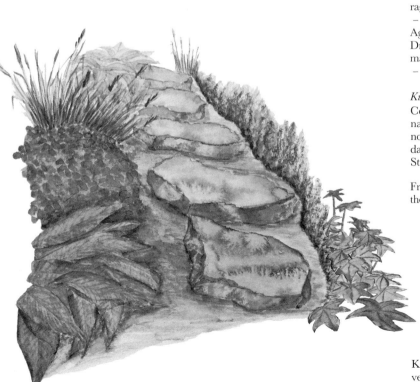

Kildare, Japanese Gardens: path of adventure

Chapter 2

County Wexford

The ruggedness and variety of landscape of Wicklow give way to undulating tilled fields in Wexford. What this county does not have in scenery it tries to make up for in sunny weather. Wexford is the 'sunny south-east' of Irish tourist brochures. Before Irish people could afford sun holidays in Spain, Wexford was the driest and sunniest place they could find. Courtown Harbour and Ballymoney are examples of holiday resorts with good sandy beaches and 'amusement arcades' for wet days.

Wexford has seen the victory and defeat of Celts, Vikings and Normans. The oldest surviving Celtic traditions in Britain and south-west Wales (Dyfed) are remnants of colonisation in AD 300 by the *Déise* tribe from the south-east of Ireland.

Colonisation was to flow the other way when the Normans crossed from Wales in 1169 to begin the long and turbulent history of conflict between Ireland and England, which is not yet concluded.

Enniscorthy

The pleasant town of Enniscorthy is built on steeply sloping ground by the river Slaney. A Norman castle, rebuilt in 1586, houses a folk museum and historical information about Wexford's part in the 1798 rising against English rule. In the summer and autumn of that year Ireland was seething with revolution. Encouraged by the French revolution Irish republicanism began to form into a political philosophy under a northern Irish presbyterian called Wolfe Tone, leader of the United Irishmen. He sought and received aid from the new Republic of France. In an effort to prematurely explode the developing revolution, English generals Lake and Johnson successfully provoked an early rebellion. The burning of the catholic church at Boolavogue, not far from Enniscorthy, caused a spontaneous rebellion in early summer 1798. After a month of bloody fighting with atrocities on both sides, the rebels were defeated at Vinegar Hill, Enniscorthy. Isolated rebellions erupted throughout Ireland, especially in Wicklow, and were systematically suppressed. When the expected French help arrived in autumn 1798 they were easily defeated. Seventy years were to elapse before another major rebellion would be attempted.

Today, a good view of the surrounding countryside with barley fields and strawberry fields may be had from Vinegar Hill. Wexford's Strawberry Fair is held every year at the end of June in Enniscorthy. When paying for your juicy strawberries, have a look at your five-pound note. You will see Mr Scotus, who was a Wexford man of some distinction a few hundred years ago...

Hook light-house, a silent sentinel over 700 years old

We took Camolin and Enniscorthy,
And Wexford storming drove out our foes,
'Twas at Slieve Coillte our pikes were reeking
With the crimson blood of the beaten Yeos.
At Tubberneering and Ballyellis,
Full many a Hessian lay in his gore,
Ah, Father Murphy had aid come over,
The Green Flag floated from shore to shore!

At Vinegar Hill, o'er the pleasant Slaney,
Our heroes vainly stood back to back,
And the Yeos at Tulluow took Father
Murphy,
And burnt his body upon a rack.
God grant you glory, brave Father Murphy,
And open Heaven to all your men,
The cause that called you may call to-
morrow,
In another fight for the Green again.

Two verses of the song 'Boolavogue'
by P.J. McCall.

A Wexford pike of the type used in the
1798 rising. The pointed top was used
like a lance, while the side piece was
used to unseat the horsemen of the English cavalry. Unfortunately the courage
of the 'pikemen' was no match for can-
nons and guns.

Wexford town

Like other towns on the east coast, Wexford was founded by the
Vikings around AD 850. The old native Irish were never urban
dwellers and it fell to the Vikings and later the Normans to build the
towns and cities. Even today there still seem to be remnants of this
early anti-urban bias in the Irish mentality.

Wexford takes its name from the Norse Waesfjord, accurately
naming it the 'harbour of the mud flats'. The names Keyser's Lane
and St Olaf's church recall the Viking presence. The existing street
patterns retain the lanes leading down to the harbour and crescent
pool where Viking ships landed. Now the statue of John Barry, who
emigrated from Wexford to America and became that country's first
navy commander during its War of Independence, looks out over the
place where Norse longboats were first moored. In the distance the
famous bird sanctuary of the Wexford slobs (or mud flats) can be
seen.

The Normans created the Bull Ring in the centre of the town. It
takes its name from bull-baiting, a cruel pastime of the Norman
nobles in earlier times. Another, more peaceful, Norman way of
passing time, was the after-dinner siesta which found local acceptance
until the middle of the nineteenth century. Similarly, a local dialect
called Yola, containing many old English and Flemish words,
survived until around the same time. The names on shops and offices
– Roche, Colfer, Deveraux, Fitzhenry – are a reminder of these
people.

Another distinctive and still surviving south Wexford tradition is
mumming. It was introduced by shipwrecked Cornish sailors and
originally consisted of miming and folk-dance with sword-play,
portraying the triumph of Good over Evil. In the nineteenth century
patriotic characters were added in the aftermath of the 1798 rebellion.

A more recent tradition is the International Wexford Opera
Festival held every October since 1951. It enjoys a good reputation
for well-performed classic opera (usually lesser-known operas) and for
the 'social' enjoyment of the many visitors. Those Irish pubs again,
no doubt!

Wexford is still the landing place and leaving point for foreigners
and Rosslare Harbour, seventeen kilometres away, is the car-ferry
port for Fishguard, Pembroke, Le Havre and Cherbourg.

At Carnsore Point, a few kilometres south of Rosslare Harbour,
the Irish government planned to build its first nuclear power plant in
the late 1970s. Thanks to public opposition and the huge projected
building costs, Ireland was spared this unnecessary and risky
development.

The Wexford slobs

Within sight of the original mud flats that gave Wexford town its Viking name are more recent mud flats or slobs, famous as bird sanctuaries. Reclaimed from the sea in the 1840s, over 1000 hectares of mud flats provide refuge for many different species of birds in winter time. The public reception area of Wexford Wildfowl Reserve, one of the most important bird sanctuaries in Ireland, provides a lecture hall, library and observation tower. The Saltee Islands, accessible from Kilmore Quay, are also renowned for their variety of bird life.

Swans and ducks in Wexford's slobs

Johnstown Castle and Gardens

South of Wexford, near Murntown, lies Johnstown Castle. It sits like a decorated Gothic cake on a green platter of gardens. Both the castle and gardens were designed by Daniel Robertson, who also was responsible for the more impressive Powerscourt Gardens in county Wicklow. Johnstown estate was donated to the State by its last owners and is now used as a soils research centre. The castle is not open to the public but the gardens and agricultural museum are open on weekdays.

Tacumshane windmill

South of Killinick signposts point to Tacumshane, a tiny village of a few houses and one shop-cum-petrol station. This shop, like most small village shops, sells bread, vegetables and meat and the owner, Mr Michael Meyler (a Norman name), has the key to one of Ireland's two surviving windmills. I went in and asked for the key, we discussed the weather and I left the shop with *The Irish Times*, some fresh fruit and the key.

   You can explore the mill and see how it worked. Built in 1846, the thatched top and sails could be moved into a windward position by means of a metal ground wheel connected to the sails by a strong timber pole. Tacumshane windmill faces out to sea, to St George's Channel where so many ships have floundered between Tuskar Rock and Hook Head light-houses.

Hook Head

On the way to Hook Head you pass Tintern Abbey, said to have been founded by William the Marshall around AD 1200 in gratitude for surviving a terrible storm in St George's Channel. Tradition claims that William made a vow to God that wherever his drifting and rudderless boat landed he would build a church.

   The peninsula of Hook is like a long tongue stuck out into the rough sea as if to tease and excite the breakers into even more intense violence. The steep sea-cliffs contain many fossilised sea shells in carboniferous limestone. The water is deep close to shore and the

Tacumshane windmill was built in 1846 and used for ninety years for grinding corn

tidal sweep around Hook Head gives rise to sudden tidal surges. Large fissures and blow holes in the cliffs stand next to the 'Tower of Hook'. This light-house dates from the thirteenth century and the internal stairs to the top of the black and white building is contained completely within the thickness of the wall.

Tradition says that a light was kept burning at this place by early Christian monks from the sixth century onwards. It is known that the Canons Regular of St Augustine were in charge of the present light-house until medieval times. To the south-west of the Hook, across on the Waterford side of the inlet is Crook Castle. In 1650 the English general Cromwell rounded the head and said he would sail up the inlet 'by Hook or by Crook' and thus the English language expression was born. Like the word 'boycott',* it was conceived in the political struggle between Ireland and England of which the Cromwellian war was one of the blackest periods... Luckily, the white light of the ancient tower still shines as it has done for 1500 years, a silent sentinel watching the coming and going of invader and emigrant.

Kennedy Park

In the late 1840s Ireland suffered a terrible famine. Within five years one million people had died and a further million had emigrated, mainly to America. The great-grandfather of US president John F. Kennedy, Patrick Kennedy, was one of those who emigrated. Within

* Captain Boycott was a landlord in nineteenth-century Ireland, whose tenants subjected him to the 'boycott'.

two kilometres of his former home in Dunganstown is a park
dedicated to the assassinated president, who only six months before
his death visited his ancestral home. With initial financial help from
Irish Americans the Irish government has developed and is
maintaining the John F. Kennedy Memorial Arboretum and Forest
Park, opened in 1968. The fine visitors' centre is made of local stone
and western red cedar and contains information about the well-
signposted walks.

Much of the landscaped park is taken up by a collection of trees
and shrubs from all over the world. At present there are about 3000
different species and varieties, but this will be doubled when the
collection is complete. Species of trees are planted in plots big enough

A steep street in the centre of New Ross. Characteristic Irish individuality is shown in the slight difference between houses of the same type, all in different bright colours.

to show how they will develop when planted as a forest crop.

The park measures 194 hectares, but a little effort will be well
rewarded if you are willing to use your legs rather than the car. If
you insist on driving, it is possible to get to a panoramic viewing
point high up on Slieve Coillte. The park is open all the year round
and during the summer you can visit the shop and café as well.

New Ross

Around the sixth century New Ross was a small settlement with a
monastery and school. When the Normans arrived it grew in
strategic importance, since it commanded the river crossing to
Waterford. William the Marshall (of the Tintern Abbey story,
remember?) built the first bridge, but later a town wall was needed to
keep Gaelic clans from capturing the town. An old ballad tells how
practitioners of the different trades, drapers, butchers and
wainwrights were required to give one day a week of free labour to
the building of the town walls. On Sundays it was the turn of the
women, who made a gate called 'Lady Gate'. This name was to
change to 'Three Bullet Gate' when Cromwell fired three cannon
shots in 1649, and the town surrendered. They had learned that

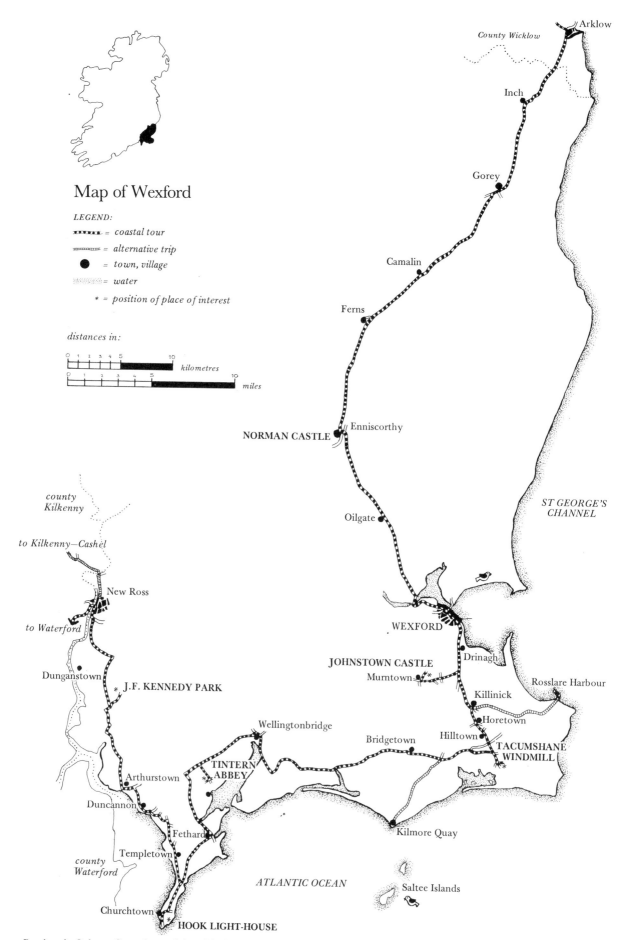

Map of Wexford

LEGEND:

- = coastal tour
- = alternative trip
● = town, village
- = water
* = position of place of interest

distances in:

0 1 2 3 4 5   10   kilometres

0 1 2 3 4 5   10   miles

County Wicklow

Arklow

Inch

Gorey

Camalin

Ferns

Enniscorthy

NORMAN CASTLE

ST GEORGE'S CHANNEL

county Kilkenny

to Kilkenny–Cashel

New Ross

to Waterford

Oilgate

Dunganstown

* J.F. KENNEDY PARK

WEXFORD

JOHNSTOWN CASTLE

Drinagh

Murntown

Rosslare Harbour

Killinick

Horetown

Hilltown

Wellingtonbridge

Bridgetown

TACUMSHANE WINDMILL

Arthurstown

TINTERN ABBEY

Duncannon

Fethard

Kilmore Quay

Templetown

county Waterford

ATLANTIC OCEAN

Saltee Islands

Churchtown

HOOK LIGHT-HOUSE

Based on the Ordnance Survey by permission of the Government of the Republic of Ireland (Permit no. 4503).

three-quarters of the population of Wexford town had been killed for resisting. Cromwell spared the people of New Ross, but they were not so lucky in the 1798 rebellion, when 3000 people were killed in ten hours of fierce street fighting.

Today, the 'Three Bullet Gate' stands close to where cars are fighting their way through the narrow streets with a logic all of their own.

Leaving New Ross you have a choice of two different routes. You may drive via Waterford, Dungarvan and Ardmore to Youghal, county Cork. Alternatively, you may travel north to Kilkenny and then south-west via Cashel, Caher and Lismore to reach Youghal.

Coastal tour county Wexford

Route descriptions correspond with map on opposite page.

Route to Enniscorthy and Johnstown Castle
Arklow – Inch – Gorey (N11) – Camolin – Ferns – Enniscorthy: Norman Castle – Oilgate – Wexford town – Drinagh – Murntown: Johnstown Castle and Gardens.

Route to Tacumshane
From Murntown to Killinick (N25) – Horetown – Hilltown – Tacumshane: windmill.

Route to Hook Head
From Tacumshane to Bridgetown (R736) – Wellingtonbridge – (R733) Tintern Abbey – Fethard (R734) – Churchtown: Hook light-house.

Route to J.F. Kennedy Park and New Ross
From Churchtown to Templetown – Duncannon – Arthurstown (R733) – J.F. Kennedy Park – New Ross (R733).
N25: Waterford city; R700: to Kilkenny.

From New Ross you have the choice of following the N25 toad to Waterford or taking road R700 to Kilkenny. Both routes are described in the next chapter.

Gate near a cottage in the small village of Tacumshane.
By the way, Wexford is the only county where you can see thatched cottages which have upper floors.

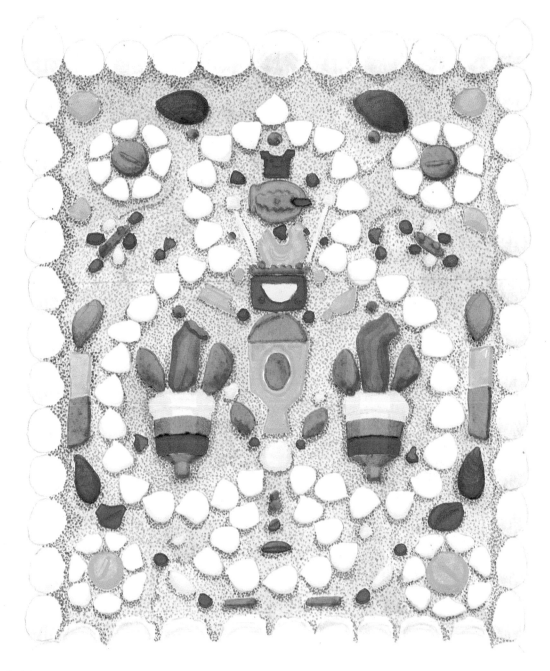

Detail of the Shell cottage, Dungarvan.
This drawing shows only a very small
part of the garden wall, about 30 cm².

Chapter 3
County Waterford

The landscape of county Waterford is somewhat more rugged than
that of Wexford. The county is traversed by two mountain ranges,
the Comeragh and the Monavullagh mountains, with their corrie
lakes and a patchwork of new evergreen forests whose rigid straight
edges could surely be softened by deciduous trees.

If you want to reach Cork and Kerry quickly, you will probably
follow the coastal tour, otherwise the alternative trip via the counties
Kilkenny and Tipperary will be a worthwhile detour. Both routes
lead to Youghal, county Cork.

Waterford city

Waterford, like Wexford, was founded by the Vikings and takes its
name from the Norse, Vadrefjord. The Vikings used Waterford as a
base to launch raids up the 'three sister' rivers (the Nore, the Barrow
and the Suir) and the city was second only to Dublin in Viking
Ireland. The oldest buildings are of Viking origin. Reginald's Tower,
called after Waterford's Viking governor, was built in 1003 and the
surviving town wall was started by Sigtryggr around 850. Both were
later taken by the Normans, who added further fortifications.

Today, the old buildings and monuments of the city are in
unflattering competition with ugly surroundings. Even the hills to the
north-west are planted with electricity supply poles. But the
landscape was not always so crudely defaced. In the _Lebor Gabala_ or
the Book of Invasions, a mythological account of the prehistory of
Ireland, Waterford is described by the first Celts as special: 'A sweet
confluence of waters, a trinity of rivers, was their first resting place:
they unloaded the women and the sensual idol.'

The present idol of Waterford city is surely its world-famous
crystal glass. It used to be possible to take a guided tour through the
factory, but this has unfortunately been replaced by a repeating video
show in the clinical reception area. However, the showroom, with a
splashing fountain and shimmering chandeliers, displays the fine
craftsmanship so much sought after, especially by American visitors
for whom money seems to flow as smoothly as the rivers.

CIE, the Irish transport company, runs a one-day return bus trip
from Dublin to Waterford in the summer, which includes a cruise
from New Ross to Waterford city. The boat luncheon is enjoyable
and offers a good opportunity to share a meal and a chat with fellow
travellers. Don't be surprised if your bus driver is pleasantly talkative
and likes a singsong on the return trip.

For those who like a waterway holiday river cruisers can be hired
for the navigable Barrow, which flows through the ancient land of the
Celtic _Déise_ tribe. Moving through the sometimes narrow river
passage and forested banks recalls the atmosphere described in the
hermit life of St Déglán of the _Déise:_

'For he was in his own dear cell which he had built himself for himself. It is between wood and water in a strait and secret spot on the sea's brink, and a clear stream flows by it from the wood to the sea, and trees gird it beautifully round about.'

Finding the Knockeen Dolmen

Touring around Ireland requires good map reading abilities. Quite often you will approach a junction and find no signpost and in the case of some national monuments signposts will actually have been removed by farmers who do not want you to trespass on their land. The Knockeen Dolmen is such a monument.

On the Tramore to Carrick on Suir road you will see the turn-off sign 'Knockeen Dolmen ½ mile'. Drive until you meet a three-forked road. Take the right fork and drive about 100 metres uphill. Opposite a large white farmhouse there is a field gate and stile. You will find the brooding Knockeen Dolmen on the far side of the field in the shadow of a hedge.

When the dolmen was built four millenia ago it must have stood in a clearing and probably marks the grave of a local chieftain. Knockeen is called a 'portal dolmen' because it has two large matching uprights emphasising the entrance and supporting the heavy capstones together with three smaller standing stones. A system of propping and levering the capstone into place is thought to have been used. There are five other megalithic monuments nearby, called the Tramore group.

The Shell cottage, Dungarvan

You may love or hate the 'Shell cottage', depending on your artistic sensitivities. The cottage is a suburban type of house, but the front and back gardens as well as all the available wall surfaces are decorated with coloured shells in various patterns. But whether you consider the results to be kitsch or art you have to admire the dedication and effort which radiates from every square centimetre!

The name of the cottage comes not only from the shells that decorate it but also from the Shell oil company. An employee of theirs started collecting shells on his many sea trips and began to decorate his garden walls while home on leave. His widow now continues their life's work. The garden walls are topped with religious knick-knacks. Below them are symmetrical almost Byzantine images containing different coloured shells juxtaposed with elements of toys and saucers. The flower beds have vases, tea-pots and small sculptures on pedestals. If you are lucky enough to be invited into the house a small showroom awaits you. Shell dolls, ashtrays and houses are on view. These souvenirs are produced on a non-commercial basis by the owner and some local handicapped people. Profits from sales go to two leper colonies in Africa. While I was absorbing all this unusual information I was asked to turn my back while the woman of the house unveiled 'something you won't find anywhere else'. When I was allowed to look I saw what looked

Entrance gate near Tramore

like an upside-down flowerpot with the Virgin Mary growing from the bottom. A wedding present, I was told, made with 'help from above'. Unfortunately these rather clichéed souvenirs don't match the standard of the shell-work in the garden, but I am not so cold-hearted as to leave without buying something from this dedicated and energetic woman who uses 'only Irish materials and none of your Hong Kong rubbish'. When she made this assertion to a visiting group recently it brought a gasp of indignation from a native of that same city, much to the speaker's embarrassment.

The Knockeen Dolmen belongs to a large group of megalithic tombs which were built for burials around 2000 BC. The word megalithic comes from the Greek *megas* (great) and *lithos* (stone) and the tombs are constructed of large stones. This sort of tomb building coincided with the first great advance in human history, when people started producing food. They kept domestic animals and grew crops instead of just collecting food from natural sources.

Ardmore monastic site

Near Ardmore village are the remains of a seventh- and twelfth-century monastic settlement founded by St Declan or Déglán. Two ogham (ancient script) standing stones testify to an even earlier pre-Christian burial place and are now located within the church for safe keeping. The Romanesque church is believed to contain part of the earlier seventh-century church in its lower portions. It has an unusual recessed west window, a pointed chancel arch and arcades on the interior wall. The really special feature of the church is the beautiful relief sculptures on the exterior of the west wall. Although badly worn by centuries of rain and sea winds they are worth a closer look. You can see Michael the Archangel weighing souls in the top row of arcades, while the two larger arches below show Adam and Eve in Paradise and the Judgement of Solomon. In the eastern part of the graveyard is St Declan's oratory. This building was re-roofed in 1716 and one of the ogham stones was found incorporated in the gable.

The well-preserved round tower of Ardmore is special among Irish round towers for its use of cut stone and projecting string courses. Inside are projecting stones with grotesque heads where once there were six platform levels. The round tower is a peculiarly Irish architectural feature, with the entrance door usually three metres above ground to which entry was gained by means of a ladder which was drawn up in times of emergency. Round towers were built by early Christian monks to provide protection from Viking and other plunderers. Food and precious objects such as manuscripts were stored in these towers for safe keeping. In the margins of such manuscripts the thoughts and fears of the monk, as he dutifully transcribed the scriptures, are often to be found. Looking out to a stormy sea on a cold winter night from the vantage point of Ardmore you could imagine why the monk Sedulius wrote in the margin of his famous St Gall Priscian (written in Ireland and subsequently brought to the Continent):

Romanesque sculptures on the exterior of the west wall of Ardmore cathedral. This lower arch on the bottom right is the least wheather-worn and shows the Judgement of Solomon and the Adoration of the Magi.

The bitter wind is high tonight
It lifts the white locks of the sea;
In such wild winter storm no fright
Of savage Viking troubles me.

Alternative routes

Kilkenny and Tipperary

If you decide to travel northwards when you leave New Ross and head for Kilkenny or in another way include this town in your tour, your efforts will be rewarded.

First you can pay a visit to Jerpoint Abbey near Thomastown, a fine monastic ruin with a typical Cistercian plan dating from the late twelfth century. The buildings are arranged around a cloister which was partly restored in the 1960s. A variety of fine sculptures depicting saints, princes and knights from the medieval period are nearby and are worth a look.

Kilkenny town and castle

Kilkenny is one of those few Irish towns, along with places like Kinsale and Westport, that have something more than *ad hoc* quaintness. This can be attributed to their architectural quality, Anglo-Irish past and present interested citizens. Kilkenny has many fine old buildings, including beautifully furnished shops and pubs with hand-crafted signs. Mixing culture with entertainment makes for double enjoyment, so I suggest a drink in Tynan's Bridge House Bar, close to John's Bridge. This is a magnificent Victorian pub with a well-designed counter, shelves, gas lamps and ceiling, which is appreciated and well maintained by its owner.

Drink is important to Kilkenny. The local Smithwicks Brewery is a large local employer, and is much frequented by groups of students and tourists in search of a free drink – as well they might with the high cost of alcoholic drinks in Ireland. The major local historical power, the Earls of Ormonde, started out as butlers, but not just any old butlers, it must be said. The Ormondes had the privilege of serving each new English queen or king their first drink of wine after the coronation service. Besides the chance to have a sip when no one was looking, the wine-butler was endowed with a very lucrative entitlement which gave him ten per cent of all the wine imported into Ireland! The first serving butler, Theobald Walter, and his family became known as the Butlers and later became the Earls of Ormonde and owners of Kilkenny Castle from 1391 until 1967. A representation of three full cups of wine stands today on each side of the castle's main door. Many a king would gulp and many a butler smile at the quarter of a million pounds paid by the British government in 1811 to compensate the Butler family for the removal of their ten per cent wine entitlement.

William the Marshall of Tintern Abbey and New Ross fame first built Kilkenny Castle between 1195 and 1207 on the site of an earlier

The well-preserved round tower of Ardmore (about AD 1200) used to have six internal timber landings which were joined by stairs. At the top was a bell to call the monks to prayer. *Cloigtheach,* the Irish name, means bell tower, although it was also used as a place of refuge.

timber fortification. The building as it now stands is a mixture of Gothic, classical and Tudor styles and is definitely worth a visit, particularly the picture gallery in the east wing. Natural light washes down from the glazed apex on Butler family portraits and gives these noble people an appropriate distinction. This hall is no blank shoe-box hung with pictures as are so many of today's galleries. Rather, the architecture is clear and an object in itself, yet does not dominate the exhibition. The floor and pleasant window seats are of warm honey-coloured oak. A well-carved double fireplace and the intricately painted roof beams add life and extra interest to the whole.

Kilkenny Design Centre

Across the road from the castle are the design workshops and retail shop of the Kilkenny Design Centre, housed in the former stables of the castle.

In the early 1960s the Irish government set up these workshops to improve Irish design standards following a study by Swedish consultants. Like many countries emerging from colonial domination Irish people then had and unfortunately to a lesser extent still have an inferiority complex, which makes them think every other developed country does things better. Being a small island at the edge

One of the four sculptured heads in the small oval room near the picture gallery of Kilkenny Castle

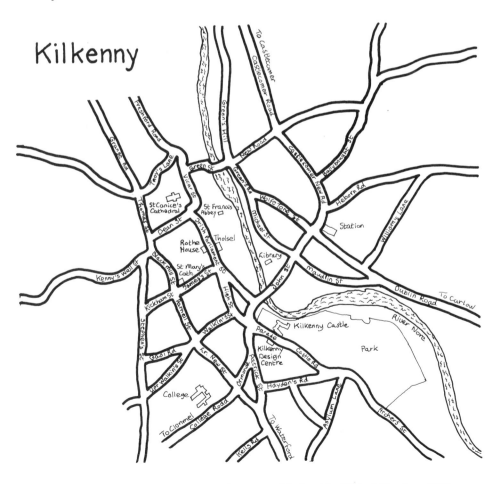

Based on the Ordnance Survey by permission of the Government of the Republic of Ireland (Permit no. 4503).

Kilkenny has an old abbey (St John's) which once belonged to the Capuchin order. Surveying the merriment of the *fleadh* you could find yourself in agreement with the Irish eighteenth-century epigram translated by Thomas Kinsella:
You who indulge in drink, in meat on Fridays, and all the pleasures from table to blissful bed, if the promise of Heavenly glory applies to you then much has the Capuchin Order been misled.

A section of a poem by the local vicar general who was put to death by Cromwellian forces in 1652 at the age of seventy-two tells of native Irish resentment against English influence. It is translated from the Irish by Thomas Kinsella.
A trick of this false world has laid me low: servants in every home with grimy English but no regard for one of the poet class save 'Out! and take your precious Gaelic with you!'

Railing with shamrock-motifs in Kilkenny town

of Europe has also contributed to an insular mentality and economic hardship forced many dynamic people to leave the country never to return. Although Ireland has accomplished a good deal in the field of modern literature the visual arts are underdeveloped and still largely seen as non-essential in this country. This is depressing for talented young artists and designers, many of whom have worked abroad and brought back valuable experience. But most of them realise that they can be as good as any foreigner, given an enlightened client.

The Kilkenny Design Centre continues to develop and encourages designers through travelling scholarships. It also acts as a sales outlet for many craft workers through shops in Kilkenny and Dublin, where you can buy well-designed pottery, glass, weaving, knitwear and much more.

Kilkenny monuments

I will not list all the monuments you could see, but rather the ones that struck me as special.

Wandering up High Street and Parliament Street, you will notice the Tholsel stepping out over the pavement with Tuscan pillars to form an arcade. It dates from 1761 and is mainly built of unpolished black marble, for which Kilkenny is famous. Formerly a toll or exchange house it is now a municipal building.

Across the road not far up the street is Rothe House which also has an arcaded street front, but is 167 years older than the Tholsel. It is a well-preserved example of a rich merchant's house from the sixteenth century. It consists of three buildings, parallel to each other but separated by two inner courtyards and joined together on one side by a linking passage. The first two houses have been restored and serve as the museum and library of the local archaeological society.

Rothe House and the name of the street, Parliament Street, are interwoven in history. It was in Rothe House that bishop David Rothe, a relative of the owner and leader of the catholic bishops met informally with other catholic leaders. This was during the period 1642-48 when Kilkenny was the headquarters of the 'Confederate Catholics of Ireland'. There was a time during the English Civil War when native Irish and Anglo-Irish catholics joined together to defend their land and religion. The Confederates supported the English King Charles I against Oliver Cromwell, because they regarded his cause as the one most likely to help their aims. At one time the Confederates controlled most of Ireland except Dublin and north-east Ulster. However, a split developed and not for the first or last time in Irish history native Irish and Anglo-Irish went their different ways to the detriment of both.

Cromwell came to Ireland to follow up his victory in England. Those Irish who were not killed during this slaughter were afterwards deported to the West Indies, while the more wealthy landowners and merchants had to move westwards. Their land and wealth became the spoils of war to be given to a new wave of loyal English settlers. In preparation for this 'plantation' of Englishmen an extensive survey of Ireland was done by Sir William Petty, called the 'Down Survey' (because all details were noted 'down'). It was the most complete set of maps to be made until the mid-nineteenth century. The fine drawings can still be seen in the National Library in Dublin.

At the top of Parliament Street stands St Canice's Cathedral from which Kilkenny takes its name from the Irish *Cill Chionnaigh*, the church of Canice. The round tower indicates that there was a religious site here before the building of the cathedral commenced around 1251. Fine stone carvings and the gallery under the west window are special features of St Canice's, extensively restored in 1864. The present stained glass design of the east window dates from the same period. It was a gift from the Butler family and its theme is the same as the former stained glass window which was destroyed by Cromwellian forces when they used the cathedral as a stable two centuries earlier.

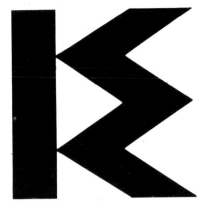

The logo of the Kilkenny Design Centre

Kilkenny events

Every year in the summer an arts week is held in Kilkenny with exhibitions in various places in the town. On one of my visits this arts week coincided with the *fleadh*, a traditional Irish music festival which is organised yearly in successive towns or villages in Ireland. So watch out for this *fleadh* (say flah) because it's great fun.

Man playing *uileann* pipes during the *fleadh*, an annual traditional Irish music festival

During the *fleadh* in Kilkenny the streets are packed with people and traffic. Family groups, friends and fellow musicians play music together in large and small groups surrounded by their audience. Complimentary terms such as 'lovely', 'good man' or 'powerful' encourage the many excellent musicians. Drifting through the crowds and struggling to get a drink or snack in any of the many pubs, you may come across very well-known traditional musicians playing away with new and old friends in some corner, surrounded by onlookers and pints of stout.

As well as the informal music sessions in the streets and the pubs there are formal competitions to choose the best musicians of different ages for various traditional instruments. A list of competitions and their location can be got at the *fleadh* office which is set up for the duration of the event. A family over from England for this festival is so delighted that their son won a gold medal, that they are telling everyone they meet how Irish and proud they feel. The little eight-year-old hero is eating double helpings of fish and chips and taunting his brothers and sisters, knowing that the day is his to glory in.

With the help of a relaxed and cigarette-smoking policeman on traffic duty I leave Kilkenny and head for Cashel. On the way a police car passes driving at high speed with only one rear light and unlighted registration plate. The reason for their hurry can be guessed, since I pass them again, their car now parked discreetly near a less crowded country pub...

The Rock of Cashel

The distinctive and boldly shaped buildings which seem to grow out of the Rock of Cashel are unique among the many religious monuments of Ireland and date from the tenth to the fifteenth century. Long before that time this limestone rock was a military and political capital for Munster (the southern province) kings and princes. Before one grey stone was added to another this place was known as *Sidh Dhruim*, meaning otherworld ridge or fairy ridge. You get that feeling of an otherworld when you survey the countryside from this vantage point.

The English name Cashel comes from the Irish word *caiseal* meaning fortress or seat of power. From the building of the first *caiseal* until the beginning of the twelfth century it is referred to as 'Cashel of the kings'.

From the fifth century onwards Cashel was also called St Patrick's Rock, as it was visited by the national saint. It appears from some historical sources that the intertwining of church and state grew until the ninth century when Feilim Mac Criomthain was considered 'king of Munster, scribe and bishop'. Echoes of modern Irish church-state relations, some night say!

The Vikings made it to Cashel but were defeated by Mac Criomthain's successor, which goes to show that he could swing a sword as well as a crosier. In the twelfth century King Murtagh O'Brien made a grant, 'such as no king before made, namely he granted Cashel of the Kings to the Religious'. By that time the round tower had already stood for over a hundred years. The remarkable St

A seventeenth-century Dominican priest/poet from Cashel, called Pádraigin Haicéad, wrote 'Do Chuala Inné' (meaning 'I heard yesterday'), an invective poem criticising the church in Ireland for forbidding monks to write poems or songs. It is believed that he was in Louvain, Belgium when he wrote these two stanzas from a longer poem. It is translated from the Irish by Thomas Kinsella.

I heard from a decent man the other day
a piece of news from the 'spouse of Conn and Corc':
that the church condemns our Gaelic's subtle paths,
the polished pleasure of our noble fathers...

I will stitch my mouth up with a twisted string
and say no word about their mean complaining,
merely condemn the herd of narrow censors
and the hate they bear my people, O my God.

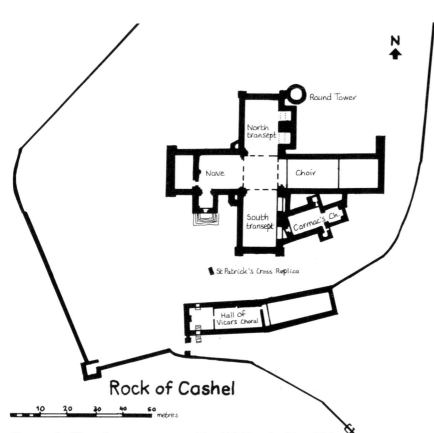

Rock of Cashel

Cormac's Chapel was consecrated in 1134 by the king-bishop Cormac Mac Carthy. Ninety years later the cathedral was begun and around 1420 the Hall of the Vicars was built.

The present entrance building or Hall of the Vicars Choral was excellently restored in the 1970s and now houses some exhibits, including St Patrick's Cross. A house of the lived-in variety had to be carefully removed from the shell of the building prior to restoration! You may come across other still lived-in or used monuments on your tour and in some ways it is refreshing not to see everything railed off and tourist packaged, especially since there are so many surviving monuments in Ireland.

St Patrick's Cross is unusual, as it has not the ring round the intersection of shaft and transom normal in Irish high crosses. It is believed that the one remaining outside frame or support was continuous around the cross. It is carved from one large block of stone and shows Christ crucified on the west face, while St Patrick is shown standing on an ox-head on the east face. The weather-worn base panel of interlaced beasts shows the influence of Irish and Viking design, as does the sarcophagus in the cathedral.

The ceiling and the oak hammer type of roof of the Hall of the Vicars are worth noting. No nails are used and only timber dowels interconnect the beams and purlins. As was the tradition of old, the architects who worked on the restoration have their initials noted on a display shield.

Outside on the rock you will see a copy of St Patrick's Cross, where the original once stood. To your right are Cormac's Chapel and the cathedral, unusually positioned in relation to one another. In

The dramatic Rock of Cashel seen from the very bottom of the hill, where the buildings seem to grow out of the rock. The series of small heads are taken from Cormac's Chapel, the large male head is from the cathedral.

times long past it was common to orientate a church to the sunrise on the feast-day of the saint to whom the church was dedicated. The cathedral dedicated to St Patrick is almost due east and agrees accurately with the sunrise on St Patrick's Day, 17 March. Cormac's Chapel dedication day falls in the month of May and is some fifteen or sixteen degrees to the north of east. The same axis alignment is shared by St Patrick's Cross, carved around the same period as the building of the chapel.

The architecture of Cormac's Chapel owes its form and detail to a marriage of Rhineland Romanesque and native Irish technology. There are documented links between Cashel and the Irish monasteries of Cologne and Ratisbon at, and before, its erection. Some years prior to the building the Irish abbot of Ratisbon sent four men to Ireland to assist in the funding and design of Cormac's Chapel. The application of native technology can be seen in the stone

roof, built on the principle of the true arch, but the bed joints of the individual stones are not inclined. The influence of Irish beehive hut design and their corbel* principle seems to have compromised the pure geometry of the true arch. A surprising feature of the chapel's plan is the eccentric position of the chancel relative to the nave. This is due to the widening of the nave on the north-western side only during the course of erection. Irish _ad hoc_ planning at work again!

Looking at the many carved heads in the chapel I could not help thinking of the Celtic head cult. While carved heads are a feature of Romanesque architecture originating in France, it is possible that both Irish and French carvings derive from Celtic prototypes, such as those found at Celtic monuments in Roqueperteuse and Entremont in southern France.

* See page 15

Coastal tour county Waterford

Route descriptions correspond with map on opposite page.

Route to Waterford city and Knockeen Dolmen
New Ross (N25) – Glenmore – Slieveroe – Waterford city – Southside (R675) direction Tramore: Knockeen Dolmen (see map)

Route to Shell cottage and Ardmore monastic site
From Knockeen to Tramore – Fennor (R675) – Bunmahon – Dungarvan: Shell cottage – Gorteen (N25) – Currach (R673) – Ardmore: Monastic site – Kinsalebeg (N25) – Youghal (county Cork)

Alternative routes

Kilkenny town
From New Ross (N79) direction Enniscorthy – (N700) Thomastown – Bennettsbridge – Kilkenny

Rock of Cashel, Cahir Castle
From Kilkenny (N76) direction Clonmel – (N691) Ballylin – Ballingarry – Killenaule – Ballinure – Cashel: St Patrick's Rock – (N8) New Inn – Cahir: Cahir Castle – (R668) Clogheen – Lismore – (N72) Tallowbridge – Tallow (R634) – Youghal (county Cork)

Cahir Castle

The site of Cahir Castle is a rock outcrop on the river Suir, dating from the fourteenth century. From 1375 it was a stronghold of the famous Butler family who controlled much of Tipperary and Kilkenny for so long.

Since the middle 1960s, when it came under state care, it has been restored and now includes an audio-visual presentation about the castle and other neighbouring monuments. The high point of my visit there was the tour given by a young guide. Her enthusiasm, energy and effort were as much a delight as was her informative tour. We were taken through the elaborate defensive outer, middle and inner wards or enclosures as if we were a group of attacking soldiers. The obstacles to our success were unfolded with clarity and vividness and there was no deluge of historical dates. The standard of guides at important Irish national monuments is high compared to the Continent. Also, Irish monuments are not ruined by souvenir shops.

KILKENNY

Bennettsbridge

Ballingarry

Ballinure

Ballylin

Thomastown

PATRICK'S ROCK

Newinn

County Kilkenny

County Tipperary

New Ross

HIR CASTLE   Caher

Glenmore

River Barrow

Clogheen

River Suir   Slieveroe

County Wexford

Waterford City

KNOCKEEN DOLMEN

Waterford Harbour

Fennor   Tramore

Bunmahon

Lismore

SHELL COTTAGE

Dungarvan

Tallow

Dungarvan Harbour

Gorteen

Map of Waterford

LEGEND:

〰️ = *coastal tour*

〰️ = *alternative trip, route*

● = *town, village*

▨ = *water*

✳

Kinsalebeg

Youghal

to Cork City   Ardmore
     MONASTIC SITE

Youghal Bay   *ATLANTIC OCEAN*

distances in:

0 1 2 3 4 5   10   *kilometres*

0 1 2 3 4   5   10   *miles*

Based on the Ordnance Survey by permission of the Government of the Republic of Ireland (Permit no. 4503).

The elongated entrance hall of Fota House has remarkable yellow scagliola pillars and Regency style plaster panels, which are subtly lit by the daylight from the high windows. The interest and friendliness of the staff create a very relaxed atmosphere and make a visit well worth while.

Chapter 4

County Cork

The Cork coast is very extended and beautiful and is dotted with many colourful and interesting towns. Youghal, Cobh, Kinsale, Skibbereen and Bantry, each has its own distinctive charm. The landscape is green, hilly and spacious in the south while the south-west is mountainous and rocky with peninsulas, bays and islands near the coast.

The Corkonians are reputed to have a strong sense of their own identity. As the Cork writer Frank O'Connor put it 'they mistrust everyone outside of their own county, especially those who come from Dublin'. More positively this local patriotism has given rise to a Cork newspaper, two locally brewed stouts, a symphony orchestra and a ballet company.

Youghal

After you cross the broad estuary of the Blackwater river you come to the seaside town of Youghal (pronounced 'Yawl'), famous for its *pointe d'Irlande* lace. Many of the houses are brightly painted and a

well-maintained nineteenth-century bandstand painted firebrigade
red catches your attention on the quays. In the nineteenth century a
developer attempted to make Youghal the Brighton of Ireland
through exploitation of its fine beach and proximity to Cork city, but
luckily for us he went bankrupt and Youghal today is a pleasant
place to vist.

In the Main Street the Clockgate Tower squats over the street.
The four-storey tower dating from 1777 is a handsome building with
an ugly record because at one time prisoners were hung from its
mullioned windows. If that thought does not put you off you can visit
the local tourist office and museum inside. You will get a good view
of the town from the top floor – that is if the office is open. The
attendant I met on a Saturday afternoon told me he kept his own
opening times! Good time keeping is not a strong Irish characteristic.

Up a steep flight of steps to the side of the Clockgate and you will
see the fifteenth-century town walls. These walls would have been
over a hundred years old when Sir Walter Raleigh returned from his
American travels. Raleigh lived in Myrtle Grove, near St Mary's
church and was mayor of Youghal in 1588. Myrtle Grove still stands
today and its Elizabethan gabled houses are locally believed to have
witnessed Sir Walter boiling the first spud (potato) followed by a puff
on the first cigarette. Certainly his spuds are ever-present in Irish
cooking today, although his cigarettes are beginning to lose favour
with a slightly more health-conscious population.

Towards the northern end of Main Street is the Red House, a fine
example of Dutch-style architecture from 1710. Two curved ramps
sweep up to the front door, which is a little too narrow for the street
elevation. Another door nearby is wide enough but it has lost its
complete elevation and is now incorporated into the façade of the
Priory Tea Shop. The original abbey doorway and new shop name
recall the Benedictine abbey which once stood here.

Alternative

Cloyne

The narrow road to Cloyne with ambush-threatening hedgerows on
both sides is an experience in itself. Roads like this and others in west
Cork were indeed used for ambushes against the English during the
War of Independence (1912-21) and again against fellow Irishmen
during the bitter and bloody Civil War which followed independence.
When I passed that way an ambush could well have taken place that
very day, to judge by the size and number of holes in the road.
There are road signs for typical Irish inconveniences such as bumps
and zig-zag corners but I propose a warning sign for potholes. It is
not the fact that the potholes are not repaired, rather it is the manner
of their repair that astonishes me. Driving along you may come
across a sign declaring, 'Major Road Works Ahead', and instead of
heavy machinery you will probably find a group of five pothole
stuffers. While one works the other four 'breast feed' their shovels but
all five will stare at every passing motorist in silent amazement. The
sole worker stuffs the hole full of tarmac and adds another shovelful

for good measure. The resulting bump is finished off with three pats of the shovel, and is then marvelled at by the whole group, before someone else takes his turn pothole stuffing.

Having narrowly missed drowning in the potholes, I arrived in Cloyne on a wet and miserable evening, the rain falling ponderously in big blobs. The round tower of Cloyne stood grey and sombre between small terraced houses. It is one of the few round towers you can climb up inside, but for that you need the key from the verger who lives opposite the tower. No one was there when I called except the barking sheep dog so I ventured to the pub and the comfort of a hot whiskey, which at least made this detour worthwhile.

Alternative

Fota estate

Fota House, surrounded by an arboretum and wildlife park, is situated on a small island in the river Lee estuary. It may not be the largest and most spectacular of Irish country houses, but it is one of the most accessible, in the widest meaning of the word. Now owned and lovingly restored by University College Cork it is a pleasure to visit. Carpets are not rolled back, nor are there any of those clumsily restraining poles and ropes so beloved of museum managements. In fact, Fota House does not feel like a museum at all; rather there is an air of relaxed pride and friendliness and the staff are eager to help.

Part of the present building was a hunting lodge, before it was extended and remodelled at the beginning of the nineteenth century by the father-and-son architectural practice of Richard and William Morrison. They remodelled the interior, added a pedimental extension on either side of the original building and built the Doric entrance portico. This is why the external views of the building are rather austere and lacking in strong composition.

However, the interior is a delight. The elongated entrance hall with its splended yellow scagliola pillars is subtly lit by the daylight streaming through the high windows. The bright soft tones and shades, the skylights over stairs and changes in direction, the repeating feature of a Greek vase and the regency style plaster panels give Fota an intimate and thoughtfully designed atmosphere. The collection of old masters hangs easily and with charm on the walls of this fine house. The drawing room looks as if the former occupiers had just gone out to the garden, leaving their pipes and books lying around.

The enclosed gardens of Fota adjacent to the rear of the house are being restored, and the collection of semi-tropical trees and rare shrubs is worth viewing. The arboretum is older than the famous Kew Gardens in London and is highly regarded by botanists. There is a very wide variety of plants and trees and you can appreciate how appropriate the word 'fota', meaning earth and warmth, really is.

You will see many places in Cork and Kerry with very lush, semi-tropical vegetation. The local micro-climate is mild owing to the influence of the Gulf Stream and frost and snow are uncommon.

This is my proposal for a new warning sign for potholes. A small percentage of Ireland's roads carry the biggest volume of traffic while thousands and thousands of kilometres of small country roads are used very infrequently, but still need repair. Without potholes, these roads can be very enjoyable and testing to drive along and you certainly will not get motorway tiredness watching out for tractors and cattle and chasing sheep dogs.

Cobh

Cobh (say Cove) owes its picturesque charm to its fine setting and well-designed buildings. The buildings at the quayside form two squares and confidently face the sea, unlike most Irish towns which turn their backs to it. The curved quayside and joyfully coloured houses put me in a holiday mood although in times past this quayside had a different more sombre mood, when it was the main departure point for Irish emigrants to America.

Casement Square ends in a pleasant courthouse with three gates, which lead to West View, a very steep street with stepped terraced houses. From the top of the hill the A-shaped slated roofs resemble their local name, 'the pack of cards', and look as if they might slide down the street if one house were removed. Luckily most houses are well maintained but some have had their characteristic bay window removed and replaced by crudely proportioned windows, a negative example of Irish personal individuality at the expense of the larger individuality of the whole street.

High on the top of the hill rises St Colman's, a Gothic Revival cathedral, its blue Dalkey granite almost white against the sky. The

West View in Cobh, called 'the pack of cards' by locals

long row of the cathedral's moulded arches seems to hold a firm grip of Cobh's soil while its outline ties the town's architecture together. If you are lucky you may hear the cathedral's forty-two bells ringing out over the bay, where sailing ships from the world's oldest sailing club still sail.

Near Cobh, on the road to Cork, there is a small museum in a former church with an exhibition of old Cobh photographs.

Cork city

Cork city and the way its people speak are special in Ireland. Frank O'Connor, Cork's best-known writer, wrote of the town: 'the up and down of it on the hills as though it had been built in a Cork accent'. It takes some time to become familiar with the Cork accent but since Cork people are not shy or short of talk, it should not take too long to discover that 'aru' means 'are you'.

There is strong rivalry between Cork and Dublin and in the 1960s this competition for first place was brought to extremes by the building of Cork County Hall, a high-rise public building just a few metres higher than Dublin's tallest building Liberty Hall on a green open site outside of Cork city! However, Cork Corporation have taken better care of their old city centre than their Dublin counterparts and have retained buildings of local and historical interest, such as the Prince's Street Market. Attempts have also been made to integrate small-scale local authority housing with private

Roof-details in county Cork, but common all over Ireland

housing unlike the Dublin practice of building vast ghettos of public housing.

Cork people today will tell you that their city is the 'real' capital of Ireland and some will remind visiting Dubliners that 'Cork' Vikings defeated 'Dublin' Vikings when they tried to take over their settlement. These 'Cork' Vikings settled on a marshy island in the river Lee which is now part of the present city centre, made irregular and picturesque by the shape of the island and the branching of the river. Take a day and walk around the city centre and absorb the atmosphere. Along the way you can absorb some Murphy's stout, Cork's answer to Guinness.

Indeed it was the locals' fondness for drink that prompted a Capuchin priest, Father Mathew to set up the temperance movement against alcoholic drink in 1838. He is remembered by a statue, a street name and a church in the city centre. When you think of the Irish fondness for downing pint after pint you can't help admiring the man for battling against the odds. It is said that a large minority of Irish people do not drink alcohol regularly but the majority that do certainly make up for them in total consumption. Ireland has a very high number of alcoholics and many of them are very young.

The pub is enshrined in Irish social life in the same way as the café is in France. It is the focus for out-of-home social activity with jokes and 'crack' flowing as freely as the beer. The great social and political issues of the day are solved as fast as the pints are consumed and when it's time to close the barman has a difficult job to clear the pub. He will start off with 'Time, ladies and gentlemen, please', progress through 'Have you no homes to go to?' until, if he is still civil, he asks 'What will you have for breakfast?'. While the pubs close early by European standards there is always someone who knows where a late night drink can be had. Adjourning to such an illegally opening pub, called a shebeen, the drinking continues in dim, often candle-lit back rooms or kitchens until the morning light. Someone is appointed to keep an ear listening for the police and any new arrival will have to give a special knock and know someone inside before being admitted.

Like the Eskimos who have so many words to describe what we would simply call snow, the Irish have a litany to describe being drunk, 'langers', 'stocious', 'spifflicated', 'twisted', 'pie eyed', or 'scuttered', to name but a few. A drunk in Ireland will be humoured, unlike his counterpart in many parts of Europe, who will be upbraided for his excesses.

A walk in Cork centre

Standing at the corner of Merchant's Quay and Patrick Street you will see the very steep Patrick's Hill rising out of the city centre while Patrick Street curves away from view. This curved shape is due to the fact that the river once flowed here and it was not until the 1780s that the present street was constructed over the still flowing river. The curve of the street and the scale of the buildings give Patrick Street a dignity and cohesion not frequently found in Irish cities.

You may wish to browse in the many shops and markets that the city centre offers and if so, try Prince's Street Market just beyond the Victoria Hotel, accessible from both Patrick Street and Grand Parade. This market has been recently restored by the city following a fire, and traditionally has been the market for meat products such as crubeens (pigs' feet), pigs' heads, tripe or black pudding. Don't make the mistake one American visitor made when she ordered black pudding, believing it to be some sort of dessert, only to find out later that it is a form of black _wurst_.

Grand Parade is the place for monumental sculptures with the 'wedding cake' Berwick fountain and Gothic canopy of the national monument. The Victorian design of the Berwick fountain is echoed in the curving shopfront of Woodford Bourne's at Patrick Street corner. The national monument stands in front of three bow-fronted, slated houses from the eighteenth century which were built from the brick ballast of visiting ships.

Looking down the South Mall you see the commercial centre of the city and another memorial, this time to the many Irish soldiers who died in British uniforms in the First World War. On the right is Father Mathew's Quay and Memorial Church picturesquely sited when viewed from up the river. From the position of the national monument, a view up the river reveals St Finbarre's Cathedral, named after the sixth-century saint who had a monastery and school here before those 'Cork' Vikings arrived. You can reach this early pointed French Gothic cathedral completed in 1880 by way of Sullivans and Bishop Proby's Quays. There is a delightful exuberance in the scale and detail of this white limestone church standing on the site of two previous churches, of which the west gateway incorporates part of the second church. While the interior does not quite match the exterior in grandness it is worth a look inside. The organ is placed six metres below floor level and a cannon ball dating from the siege of Cork in 1690 is on display in the south transept. It comes from the first medieval church destroyed during that siege. You may sit down and rest your legs while admiring the details that take your fancy considering your next move. You can walk out towards University College Cork (UCC) via Gill Abbey Street and return towards the city and Washington Street via the Mardyke Walk, or you can go directly via Crawford and Hanover Street to Washington Street and Bachelor's Walk.

The campus of UCC is a pleasant place. The oldest buildings are from 1849 in Tudor Gothic, but in the northern enclosed cloister there is a collection of ancient ogham stones worth a look. Ogham is a form of early Celtic writing in a code carved with strokes on the edge of a stone pillar. The Greek writer Lucian, who wrote in the second century AD, tells us that the Celts in Gaul (France) called their god of eloquence Ogmios. He also describes the symbolically painted scene of Ogmios as an old man clad in a loin cloth, with a group of followers whose ears are attached to his tongue by gold and amber chains. The pagan god Ogma of the Irish Celts is believed to derive from its continental counterpart and is traditionally credited with the invention of the Ogham letters.

Behind the redbrick biological institute is Horan Chapel, a 1915 attempt at twelfth-century romanesque, based on Cormac's Chapel at Cashel. As an interpretation of how a twelfth-century church

'Partly coloured like the people, red and white is Shandon steeple' goes a well-known Irish ditty about this church in Cork city, built of white limestone and red sandstone

*Based on the Ordnance Survey
by permission of the Government
of the Republic of Ireland
(Permit no. 4503).*

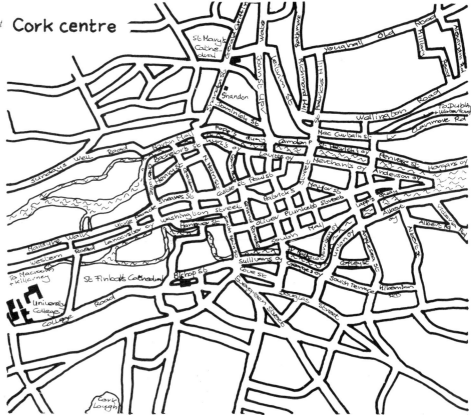

Cork centre

might have been it is worth visiting and it even has a representation of a round tower in the north transept. There is an unhurried air about UCC not found in Dublin colleges.

It is enjoyable to return to the city via the Mardyke Walk, from which you can gain access to Fitzgerald Park and the city museum. On a sunny afternoon, the Mardyke and the river will give you time to pause and reflect as you come into the last third of your tour. Along Bachelor's Quay there are some elegant Georgian houses while the North Mall's bridges and tree-lined quay lead on to Shandon Street. As you begin your climb you will see a sign for the famous Blarney Castle, eight kilometres from Cork. This castle is a mecca for tour buses and those who wish to kiss the Blarney Stone, said to give 'the gift of the gab' or eloquence. If you want to know how the word 'blarney' came to mean pleasant talk intended to deceive without offending, here is the story. It seems that the local Irish chieftain MacCarthy pretended to agree with the English lord deputy about submitting to the English method of succession rather than the clan system of election. However, when MacCarthy failed to fulfill his promises made 'with fair words and soft speech', Queen Elizabeth I declared in frustration, 'this is all blarney.'

A little further up Shandon Street you come to Church Street and the famous Shandon tower known locally as the 'four-faced liar'. It seems the four clocks never agreed and the quickness of the Cork tongue did the rest. While you are checking out the accuracy of the local name notice how accurate and sensible the designer was in using hard-wearing white limestone on the south and west sides and

These bow-fronted, slated houses at Grand Parade in Cork city were built in the eighteenth century with the brick ballast of visiting ships. To the right is the national monument.

red sandstone on the less exposed north and east sides. The tower has eight bells which are the subject of a well-known Cork song.

Nearby is the old butter market building and further up the hill is the clumsy St Mary's Cathedral or North Chapel as locals call it. Behind the cathedral is Church Avenue, a narrow street with brightly painted tiny cottages, and below it is Roman Street with short, stepped terraces. From here make your way downhill to the river and Leitrim Street. At the corner of Leitrim Street and Patrick's Hill you are almost back where you started. From here people watched in terror when in December 1920 British paramilitaries burnt Patrick Street, the City Hall and library in reprisals for ambushes during the struggle for independence.

Close by MacCurtain Street commemorates Thomas MacCurtain republican lord mayor of Cork killed by police that same year.

The ogham alphabet is the earliest form of writing known in Ireland, probably dating from AD 300. The central line is the edge of the stone. The inscriptions are read from the bottom upwards and sometimes continue down the other side.

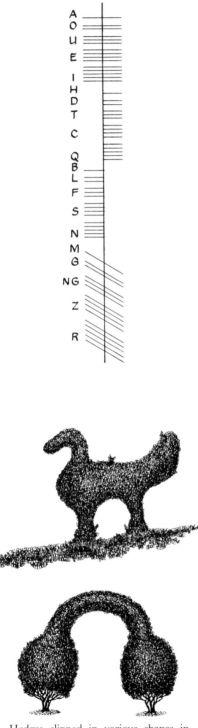

Hedges clipped in various shapes in Kinsale

Indeed 1920 saw the death of another republican lord mayor of Cork, after a hunger strike of seventy-four days in protest against British government policies in Ireland. Before his death Terence Mac Swiney said that it was not those who could inflict the most suffering who would triumph but rather those who could endure most. The Irish today, especially in Northern Ireland, are still enduring their history.

Kinsale, Charles Fort

Kinsale, thirty kilometres south-west of Cork, was the scene of an important battle in 1601. That year was a turning point in Irish history and culture. Throughout the previous century English rule had been re-established and consolidated in Ireland and began to spread outside walled towns and cities. As a result, the native Irish chieftains and their Gaelic culture were undermined. In the 1590s two Ulster Irish chieftains, O'Neill and O'Donnell, joined forces against English domination and a nine-year war ensued. In late 1601 their long-sought help from Spain arrived, but it landed in Kinsale, not in Ulster. The Irish chieftains were obliged to leave their stronghold in Ulster and march south to help the Spaniards who were surrounded by a large English army. The Irish and Spanish lost and six years later the Irish leaders fled from Ulster. Their lands were confiscated by the crown and protestant settlers from Scotland and England were brought over to ensure such an uprising would not occur again.

The problems of Northern Ireland today spring from this 'plantation' of protestant settlers and the dispossession of the native Irish, who never accepted this situation. With the flight of the Ulster chieftains went the old Irish aristocratic system of cultural patronage with drastic consequences for literature in Irish. One of those Ulster poets describes the Ireland of 1607:

Her chiefs are gone. There's none to bear
Her cross or lift her from despair,
The grieving lords take ship. With these
Our very souls pass overseas.

Kinsale town is still English in character, despite the use of Spanish names on pubs and restaurants. Indeed the specialist restaurants of Kinsale are much visited by foreigners and the more wealthy people of Cork city. Kinsale is also famous for sea fishing and boating and as a result it has become very touristy. It is still worth a visit because of its narrow streets, slate-hung houses and fine sea views. Kinsale got its town charter from Edward III in 1333 and the old courthouse dating from the seventeenth century houses a town museum with artifacts from that period until the present day.

Some three kilometres east of Kinsale lies the tiny village of Summercove and the impressive seventeenth-century Charles Fort, standing guard over the entrance to Kinsale harbour. It is a virtually unaltered star-shaped fortification with a large moat on its landward side and walls over twelve metres high. There are five bastions and from the seaward side you can see the 1603 James Fort on the other side of the estuary. It was here that William Penn's father worked as governor of Kinsale, while William worked as clerk of the Admiralty Court. Later he was given a grant of land in America on which he founded the state of Pennsylvania.

Inside Charles Fort there are a number of ruined nineteenth-century buildings of which the guardhouse and barrack stores, to the right of the entrance, have a pleasing and simple architectural quality. The ordnance sheds to the left are restored and hold a photographic and historical exhibition about the fort. It is intended to restore the better quality architectural buildings from the last century for further exhibition use, the well-informed guide told me.

Until the early 1970s this fort was neglected and one bastion was in danger of collapse. Thanks to local efforts, two international workcamps and architectural interest, the state has undertaken a programme of repair and restoration of what is a unique military monument in Ireland's eventful and vividly remembered history.

Clonakilty, Ballydehob, Skibbereen

As you move into west Cork you will see many colourfully painted towns set among landscape that becomes more and more rugged and beautiful with each kilometre travelled. Towns such as Clonakilty, Skibbereen, Ballydehob, Bantry and Glengarriff have their own stories to tell. Clonakilty was known in the past as 'Clonakilty – God help us', because it was once a dull town in an economically depressed region.

Close to the town the famous Irish War of Independence resistance leader, Michael Collins, was born in 1890. From after the rebellion of 1916 until his death in the Civil War in 1922 he was a man of great organisational ability. Despite some 60,000 British troops, paramilitaries, a large police force and martial law, Collins not alone evaded arrest but organised a guerilla war which brought the British Empire to the negotiating table. The British were to lose their first colony in what was to herald the break up of the worlds largest empire. The Indian leader, Nehru, acknowledged Ireland's example in his country's struggle for freedom in the late 1940s.

Frank O'Connor wrote about Collins's tragic death in an ambush not so far from where he was born: 'The greatest oak in the forest has crashed; it seemed as if it must destroy all life in its fall. It did destroy the *Sinn Féin* movement and all the high hopes that were set on it, and a whole generation of young men and women for whom it formed a spiritual centre.' That O'Connor, who had taken the opposite side to Collins in the Civil War, could write this, shows the great respect in which the 'Big Fellow' was held by political friends and foes alike. Clonakilty's other famous person was Henry Ford who set up the Ford car corporation after emigrating to America in the nineteenth century.

Today Clonakilty is a brighter place and the gateway to west Cork. Between Clonakilty and Skibbereen, near the village of Rosscarbery, is Drombeg stone circle consisting of seventeen standing stones. A cremated body was discovered in the centre of the circle when it was excavated. Nearby are two round huts joined together

After the Battle of Kinsale in 1601 the Irish leaders from Ulster had to flee to the Continent and Gaelic culture started to deteriorate.

Irish colleges of learning were set up in Spain, France, Italy and the Low Countries. The Irish college at Louvain became a centre of Irish learning and precious manuscripts were collected. The first printed books in Irish were published there, using this special Gaelic typeface adapted from written manuscripts.

ábcɗéꝼ
ᵹílṁnó
ꝑRꞅꞇúꞃ

Chimneys in county Cork, common in Ireland

and a cooking place. It is thought that this hilltop was a centre for hunting some two thousand years ago.

From Skibbereen you can detour to Baltimore, which not only has a beautiful coast road but also gives you the possibility of a boat trip to the unspoilt islands of Sherkin and the Irish-speaking Cape Clear. Baltimore is now a sailing centre but back in 1631 Algerian pirates sailed into town and carried off the population of some hundreds to slavery in North Africa. 'Can you imagine the poor, freckle-skinned Irish turning lobster pink under the Algerian sun; it doesn't bear thinking about,' said an old local whose son sported a fine Spanish suntan – sun cream technology no doubt.

Ballydehob is to Ireland what Timbucktoo is to the rest of the world. Few people know that it really exists but many people say it to express 'someplace in the back of nowhere'.

Bantry House

Just as you arrive in Bantry town you will see on your right side the entrance gate to Bantry House. Dating from 1750 it is built in a beautiful setting with fine views of the bay. Like many other country houses, it has seen better days but the present owner tries to make visitors welcome and gives you a typed explanation, in the language of your choice, of the house, room by room. On the chilly wet day I was there, a fire was blazing and fine classical music wafted through the hall. The original house and later nineteenth-century additions are not of such great architectural distinction as other houses of its time such as Russborough in Wicklow, but Bantry House has a famous collection of mainly French tapestries from the Gobelin, Beauvais and Aubusson workshops. From the library you see a flight of steps rising to the crest of the hill from which you have a splendid view, especially if the garden is in its beautiful autumn colours.

It was a combination of weather and good luck which gave the forefathers of the present owner the status of local lord and master. In December 1796 a group of revolutionary United Irishmen convinced France to send military help to Ireland. A fleet of forty-three ships and 16 000 men sailed from Brest but storms along its route dispersed the fleet and only sixteen ships reached Bantry Bay. The former owner of Bantry House organised a local militia and notified the British military commander in Cork. Storms and a north-east wind prevented the French from landing for five days and false news of British troop strengths caused the ships to return home. The United Irishmen's leader, Wolfe Tone, wrote in his diary, 'We were close enough to toss a biscuit ashore.' Two and a half days later a further fifteen French ships arrived but in the bad weather they had missed the previous section of the fleet and after waiting six days they too set sail for France. The owner of Bantry House was made Lord Bantry in recognition of his help against the French.

Bantry town has a pleasant vertical pattern to its street facades and some good fish restaurants in the neighbourhood of the town.

Glengarriff/Garinish

The drive from Bantry to Glengarriff is a taste of the rugged
landscape and exotic plants and trees you will find in this part of
Ireland. The Irish name for Glengarriff means rugged glen and long
walks in the nearby state forests and surrounding countryside are a
pleasure. Less of a pleasure is the ignorant behaviour of the
Glengarriff boatmen who chase you down the street in an effort to
convince you to take their boat trip to Garinish Island. I am sure
their pathetic running and shouting puts more people off the idea of
making the crossing than it bullies into going. It is a pity since
Garinish is worth visiting because of its Italian Garden, the Caseta
and Temple.

When the French navy were in Bantry Bay, Garinish Island had
only heather and gorse growing on its sphagnum peat and blue shale
soil. Now it has a lush collection of rare and interesting trees, shrubs
and flowers from all over the world. The almost sub-tropical micro-
climate of mild winters and heavy rain have helped the creation of
Mr Bryce's 'dream garden'. Up to 1910 this island was barren,until

A Palladian gate leading to the out-
houses of Bantry House

Coastal tour county Cork

Route descriptions correspond with map on opposite page.

Route to Cork City
Youghal – (N25) – Killeagh – Castlemartyr – Midleton – *alternative 1:* (R629) Ballynacorra – Cloyne: round tower – Midleton – (N25) Carrigtohill – *alternative 2:* (R625) Fota Island: Fota House and Wildlife Park – (R624) Cobh – (N25, N8): Cork city centre.

Route to Charles Fort, Bantry House
From Cork centre to Fivemilebridge (R600) – Belgooley – Kinsale – Summer Cove: Charles Fort – (R600) Kinsale – Ballinspittle – Timoleague – Clonakilty – (N71) Ross Carbery – (R507) Drombeg Stone Circle – Leap (N71) – Skibbereen – *alternative 3:* (R595) Baltimore: Cape Clear – Skibbereen – (N71) Ballydehob – Bantry: Bantry House – Glengarriff: Garinish Island – (N71) Kenmare (county Kerry).

the Scottish politician Arran Bryce bought the property and set about transforming the island. He was very interested in architecture and horticulture and commissioned the architect Harold Peto to design a mansion with an exotic Italian garden. For over three years nearly a hundred men worked on the garden, Caseta and Temple. The First World War halted work and financial restrictions did not permit the building of the mansion. The wife and son of Arran Bryce continued work on the gardens after his death in 1924 until 1953 when it was bequeathed to the nation. The hand of human endeavour and inventiveness is to be seen throughout the island which is well maintained by the Office of Public Works. On a sunny day standing on the veranda of the Caseta you could almost think you were in Italy.

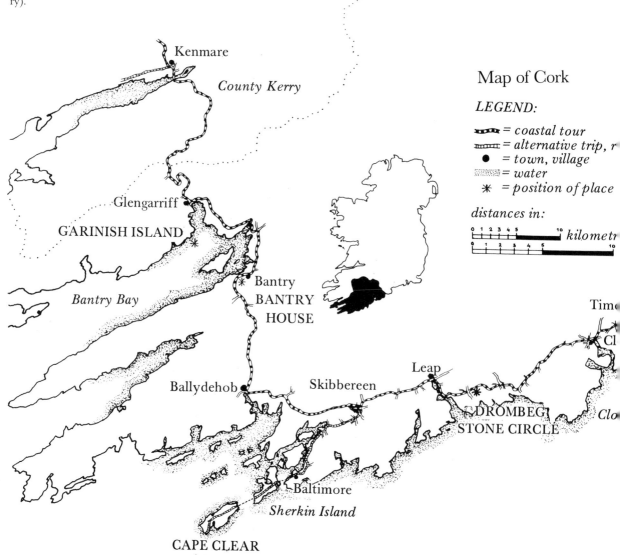

Map of Cork

LEGEND:

- ▬▬▬ = *coastal tour*
- ▭▭▭ = *alternative trip, r*
- ● = *town, village*
- ░░░ = *water*
- ✳ = *position of place*

distances in:

kilometr

Kenmare

County Kerry

Glengarriff

GARINISH ISLAND

Bantry
BANTRY
HOUSE

Bantry Bay

Tim

Cl

Leap

Ballydehob

Skibbereen

DROMBEG
STONE CIRCLE

Clo

Baltimore

Sherkin Island

CAPE CLEAR

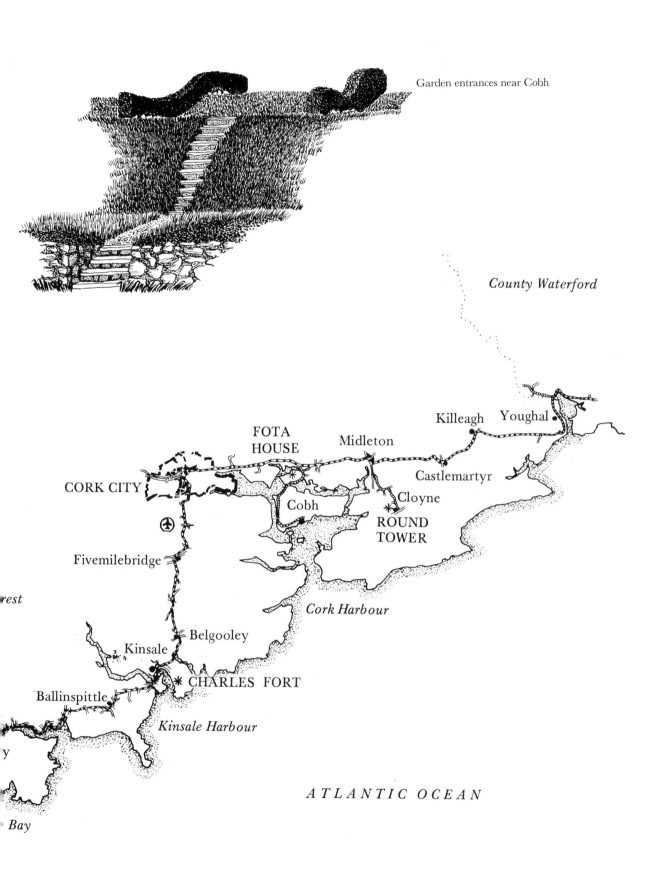

Garden entrances near Cobh

County Waterford

Killeagh   Youghal

FOTA
HOUSE   Midleton

Castlemartyr

CORK CITY

Cobh   Cloyne

ROUND
TOWER

Fivemilebridge

Cork Harbour

rest

Belgooley

Kinsale

CHARLES   FORT

Ballinspittle

Kinsale Harbour

y

Bay

ATLANTIC   OCEAN

Based on the Ordnance Survey by permission of the Government of the Republic of Ireland (Permit no. 4503).

Chapter 5

County Kerry

Kerry is a county of great beauty with a fine collection of ancient monuments, and, in places, nature's beauty is harnessed to make money from tourism. It is also a county of contrasts – Killarney's blunt commercialism is a far cry from Dingle's heritage exhibition and there are prosperous and commercially successful areas as well as

Near Killarney many georgeous views can be had, but the most famous one is Ladies' View, which is depicted here. The little lady gazing at all this beauty has come over with her family for an outing. She has just made her First Holy Communion and wears her white lace outfit with much grace.

areas of great poverty.

Historically, many Kerry people migrated to Dublin to join the civil service. Today, Kerry Gaelic football supporters frequently journey to Dublin in late September to win the all-Ireland championship final, often against the home team. The only consolation their defeated rivals can have is the numerous 'Kerryman' jokes, in which the supposedly less-than-bright Kerryman is the butt of all the humour.

Kerry is also a county for festivals. The Pan-Celtic festival is held in Killarney in mid-May, Listowel Writers' Week in May/June, Killorglin Puck Fair in mid-August and the Rose of Tralee festival at the end of August, beginning of September.

The Dingle peninsula and particularly the Irish-speaking area is memorable and long may it remain so, against the rising tide of canned tourism and crass commercialism.

The Ballyferriter Co-operative is owned by local people who wish to develop their area economically while still retaining their language and customs. They have reclaimed 3000 hectares of land, established a nursery for potted plants and also run Irish language summer courses. Their office in Ballyferriter village will arrange accommodation and tell you everything about the local area in Irish or English.

A choice of tours

You can make a choice of tours starting at Kenmare, depending on the time you have available. The main route is the more conventional one but it would be very rewarding to combine the two tours and capture the beautiful and the poetic.

Kenmare

The road from Glengarriff to Kenmare is special. You journey through buttresses of rock, expanses of bog, a patchwork of fields at the bottom of striae* strewn mountains and glimpse corrie lakes gouged out of mountain tops. Beautiful views can be had of Bantry Bay as you climb out of the lush greenness of Glengarriff into the ice-carved mountains on route to Kenmare.

The Irish name for Kenmare, *An Neidín*, means, 'the little nest', which is a good description of this pleasant place. Many Dutch people have made it their 'little nest' by converting old farmhouses to holiday homes. There is even a Dutch restaurant, run by a Dutchman and his American wife, but from my experience there they could do with a more relaxed manner and some Irish hospitality. The foreigners seem to be accepted by the Irish and friendships vary according to personality but the direct question, 'What do you think of the Dutch buying your land?' brings forth that curious but defensive rhetorical answer, 'Well that depends, but why do you ask?' Directness is not an Irish feature, although in Northern Ireland bluntness is seen as a virtue, and 'a spade is called a spade'.

The route from Kenmare to Killarney climbs and twists its way to the top of Peakeen mountain and through a narrow passage called Moll's Gap you get your first glimpse of Killarney's valley and lakes. It is extraordinarily beautiful and as you descend elements of the grand view unfold.

Numerous writers including Tennyson have sung the praises of Killarney and today the locals make it pay in tourist money. While the hard sell tactics do not quite reach the tormenting level of the Glangarriff boatmen you can be unlucky in this money-conscious town. But it would be a pity to let the commercialism put you off the beauty of the place. It can actually be enjoyable to take a pony ride or a jaunting car or, better still, a boat trip on the lake to see the area. Renting a bicycle is another less expensive way of visiting the

Entrance gate near Tralee

* Striae are scratches in the rocks which are of glacial origin

many beauty spots worth seeing – weather permitting, of course.

Killarney

The descent from Moll's Gap to Killarney town has many picturesque views and places of interest worth a second glance. Torc waterfall, which you meet after your main descent, is enjoyable to climb and the view from the top will not disappoint. You will have noticed that much of the valley is wooded and you will be pleased to know that it is a national park. The heart of this park is Muckross House, a Tudor-style house completed in 1843. The yellow Portland stone was brought by boat from England to Kenmare and then by horse and cart over the mountains to Killarney. It is just as well that jaunting car prices did not apply then or only part of the house would have been built. The Irish nation did not have to pay anything for the house and estate when the American, Bourne Vincent, presented it as a gift in 1932, after having owned the house for only thirty-one years.

The house is appropriately furnished in a Victorian manner which would have pleased the not so easily amused Queen Victoria, who once stayed here while visiting her 'loyal' subjects.

This house and lands have had a long imperial past. The Herbert and Browne families were granted the area of Killarney by Queen Elizabeth I and over the years developed their town and estates. The local poet O'Rahilly lost his traditional Gaelic patron and grant of land that went with such a position. His new lord, Valentine Browne, tolerated him only as a tenant farmer and would not restore to him, on request, his former privileges. O'Rahilly retorted with his pen:

> _A mist of pain has covered my dour old heart_
> _Since the alien devils entered the land of Conn;_
> _Our Western Sun, Munster's right ruler, clouded_
> _– There's the reason I'd ever to call on you,_
> _Valentine Browne._

(translated from the Irish by Thomas Kinsella)
The locals have regained their losses and Muckross House contains a folk museum and tea room. A blacksmith, a weaver and other artisans practise their skills for you to view in the old farm buildings.

An exhibition celebrates the skills of Kerry Gaelic footballers whose dominance of Irish football (different from soccer or rugby) is a source of local pride. However, the exhibition assumes you know all about Kerry footballers and the display of old football boots, socks and jerseys belonging to famous players is more amusing than informative.

Muckross Abbey is situated in the grounds of the estate and was the home of a Franciscan friary for two hundred years before dispossession by the Cromwellians in 1652. An old and very large yew tree stands in the centre of the cloister, which has a different proportion on each side indicating different periods of completion. With that dogged tenacity so characteristic of Irish resistance to colonisation, the Franciscans never left Killarney and in 1864 built another friary, somewhat reminiscent of Muckross Abbey, in

Female modesty
Some seventeen kilometres south-west of Killarney, on the road to Cork, are twin hills known locally as 'The Paps'. The Irish name, _Dá Chich Anann_ meaning the 'The Two Paps of Anu' refers to the pagan goddess Anu or Danu, mother of the pagan Irish gods. The curvaceous shapes brought forth the joking comment 'I think the mountains ought to be taught a little modesty' from James Stephens, the Irish writer of whom Joyce thought so highly.

Train Times
The Great Southern Hotel, originally the railway hotel, is adjacent to Killarney train station. The site for the hotel was donated to the railway company by the local earl in the mid-nineteenth century, on the strict condition that certain trains waited for him.

The Voyage of St Brendan was a very popular story in the Low Countries and Germany in the twelfth century. Brendan was a very pious Irish monk who lived in the sixth century and is reputed to have started his famous 'Journey to the Promised Land' from Fenit, county Kerry. These three drawings illustrate the beginning of the journey where the boat leaves Ireland and reaches a high, rocky island with many streams where the monks find the uninhabited house. Later they cook a meal on the back of Jasconius, a whale they think is an island.

The journeying continues along with miraculous meals, fears and wonders on many beautiful islands. Some of them are identified with existing islands in the Atlantic Ocean, thus supporting the theory that St Brendan reached America long before Columbus did.

Killarney town. It contains a fine stained glass window by Harry Clarke.

On the outskirts of Killarney is Ross Castle, a sixteenth-century tower surrounded by a bawn. It was severely damaged in the Cromwellian war and only surrendered when a ship, constructed in Kinsale, was brought overland and launched on Killarney lake. Locals say that act fulfills a prophecy which stated that the castle could never be taken except by warship. Much of the castle has been restored and on a pleasant evening a walk along the lakeshore at this point is lovely.

Killarney town is all about tourism and money and if you find that offensive there are many nice guesthouses just out of town which will suit you better.

On the north-west side of Killarney, on the Killorglin road, you turn off for the Gap of Dunloe. Near Dunloe Castle there is a group of ogham stones recovered from a destroyed souterrain. Further south at the entrance to the gap is Kate Kearney's cottage. Tradition has it that Kate was a witch. Now the cottage is greatly enlarged with a fiendish brew of coffee and a concoction of souvenirs.

The road becomes a dirt track from here and the tradition is to hire a pony. The ponies are so traditional that they return home of their own accord after completing their programmed route. You can drive through the beautiful Gap of Dunloe, in good weather, and emerge on the road one kilometre west of Moll's Gap. If you decide to drive leave it until after six or seven in the evening as the horse traffic will not let you pass. The same attitude has prevented the road from being properly surfaced because cars are seen as a threat to horse and cart tourist earnings.

Journey to the Promised Land of the Saints

The uninhabited house

Loud sounds reverberate very well in the ice-worn mountains and don't be surprised if you hear bugles echoing. It is a tradition of the Browne family now retained for the tourist, but it is special to hear the 'echoes flying'. Tennyson described the original Browne version:

The splendour falls on castle walls
And snowy summits old in story:
The long light·shakes across the lakes,
And the wild cataract leaps in glory.
Blow bugle, blow, set the wild echoes flying,
Blow bugle, answer, echoes, dying, dying, dying.

Killarney is a beautiful place so don't let its commercialism put you off. Either enjoy the well-learnt stories of the jarveys and boatmen or make your own tour but don't pass it by.

Tralee

Tralee is a lively town and the home of the national folk theatre, *Siamsa Tíre*. Their show consists of a series of Irish country traditions acted in song, music, dance and mime.

Tralee has a more recent tradition, a beauty contest to choose the Rose of Tralee at the end of August. The 'lovely ladies', I was told, are not judged on their 'beauty alone' because the well-known song tells us:

Yet 'twas not her beauty alone that won me,
Oh no, 'twas the truth in her eyes ever dawning,
That made me love Mary, the Rose of Tralee.

This festival brings entrants, who must be of Irish ancestry, from all

Snakes in Kerry
St Patrick, the national saint, is credited with driving snakes out of Ireland and sure enough none exist today. Tradition claims that St Patrick drowned the last snake in the Black Lake near the Gap of Dunloe and as a result it is now without any fish.

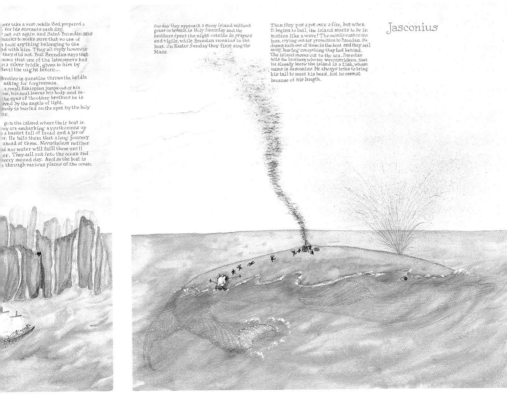

Jasconius

Ardfert village contains a collection of interesting churches dating from the twelfth to the fifteenth century. Old records mention a round tower but nothing remains of it today. The imposing ruins of the cathedral contain an Irish Romanesque west door and an effigy of a medieval bishop.

over the world to Tralee. For six days and nights organised and impromptu music and song hold forth in pubs that never seem to close. Horse races, donkey derbies, Irish dancing and marching bands fill in the side shows until the Rose is picked and the week-long hangover is put away for another year. My source on the 'lovely ladies' told me: 'I don't mind if she [the Rose] has buck teeth, it's the drink and crack I'm after.'

Fenit

Some twelve kilometres west of Tralee is the tiny port of Fenit. St Brendan the navigator is reputed to have sailed from here and discovered North America in the early sixth century. He didn't set out to find America, but the 'promised land of the Saints'. There were no Christian martyrs in Ireland, but a monk could gain sainthood by undertaking special pilgrimages or journeys into the unknown, under Christ's protection. This led to a great exodus of Irish monks to continental Europe and to St Brendan undertaking his many voyages. The story of St Brendan became very popular in the medieval period and was translated into many languages. It inspired Tim Severin to undertake his 'Brendan Voyage' in 1976, made in a replica of an Irish boat of the sixth century, which did reach Newfoundland. Severin's boat is on display in Craggaunowen, county Clare. In turn, Severin's voyage inspired Shaun Davey to compose a beautiful orchestral suite for Irish *uileann*** pipes entitled 'The Brendan Voyage'; a record definitely worth buying.

Staigue Fort, built only of unmortared dry stone, shows an inward slope of the wall-faces which gives it structural strength

*** Uileann means 'of the elbow'.*

Alternative route

Staigue Fort

The road from Kenmare to Sneem is very pleasant. Fifteen kilometres beyond Sneem there is a signposted right hand turn-off for Staigue Fort. A very narrow road climbs steeply between hedgerows and stone walls before the circular stone fort rises out of a field on your right side. A large bank and ditch surround the fort whose high walls are four metres thick and enclose an area twenty-seven metres across. A series of criss-crossing steps gives access to the top of the walls. There is a tremendous primitive strength about this pagan Celtic place.

Looking out to sea, you can relive the mythological/historical story of the coming of the Celts preserved in the twelfth-century manuscript, the *Lebor Gabala*. After journeying to Spain the Celts built a tower from which they viewed Ireland, and set out by boat to land on this Kerry peninsula. They reached the mainland on 1 May, their feast of Beltine (Gaelic tine means 'fire' and Belenus was an ancient Celtic god). Their poet Amhairghin put his right foot on Irish soil, and sang a poem in which he claims to be the origin of creation without whom nothing exists. Parallels have been drawn with the Indian god Krishna in the Bhagavad-Gita who makes similar claims such as: 'I am the ocean among the waters.'

That the Celts, an Indo-European race of people, could have preserved such links with their distant past, speaks strongly for their oral tradition, which survived their journeying through Europe to Ireland. It was eventually written down, in scarcely modified form, by Christian scribes.

Jung saw such myths as a 'treasure house of archetypal forms'. An archetypal form of more modern origin may await you back at the field gate. The farmer on whose land you have walked may seek financial compensation. A friend from Belfast refused to pay and the irate farmer showed his ignorance of accent as well as his prejudice when he told him to 'get out of here, you bloody Dubliner!'

Caherdaniel

Continuing your journey westwards you come to Caherdaniel village. Just beyond the town is Derrynane House and park, once the house of Daniel O'Connell, which is open to the public.

O'Connell is famous for his work in achieving catholic emancipation in 1829. Up until that date Irish catholics could not sit in parliament or hold public office. O'Connell was from a well-off family and because catholics were not allowed their own schools, he went abroad to France at the time of the French Revolution. What he saw there turned him against revolution and towards constitutional politics. He became a barrister and with the Catholic Association organised huge public meetings demanding emancipation. The English prime minister Wellington, of Waterloo fame, granted catholic emancipation but added a sting to its tail. Voting eligibility depended on property value and this was raised

---

The song of Amhairghin
Fain we ask Erinn,
Faring o'er ocean's
Motions to mountains,
Fountains and bowers,
Showers, rills rushing,
Gushing waves welling
Swelling streams calling
Falling foam – thunder,
Under lakes filling:
Willing – (abiding
Riding rounds, holding
Olden fairs sweetly) –
Fleet to lift loyal
Royal kings' towers,
Bowers for crowning;
Frowning foes over –

I am a stag: of seven times
*   a flood: across a plain*
*   a wind: on a deep lake*
*   a tear: the sun lets fall*
*   a hawk: above the cliff*
*   a thorn: beneath the nail*
*   a wonder: among flowers*
*   a wizard: who but I*
sets the cool head aflame with smoke?

I am a spear: that rears for blood
*   a salmon: in a pool*
*   a lure: where poets walk*
*   a boar: ruthless and red*
*   a breaker: threatening doom*
*   a tide: that drags to death*
*   an infant: who but I*
peeps from the unhewn dolmen arch?

I am the womb: of every holt
*   the blaze: on every hill*
*   the queen: of every hive*
*   the shield: for every head*
*   the grave: of every hope.*
(adapted translation from the Irish by Robert Graves)

During the tithes dispute the London *Times* wrote of O'Connell:
Scum condensed of Irish bog
Ruffian, coward, demagogue,
Boundless liar, base detractor,
Nurse of murderers, treason's factor.

from £2 to £10, thus depriving the Catholic Association of most of its voters and so rendering it politically powerless.

In the 1840s O'Connell attempted to gain a separate parliament for Ireland but English resistance and the Great Famine killed that idea. The limited success of O'Connell's constitutional approach encouraged later Irishmen to adopt a more revolutionary approach.

The Skelligs

At Caherdaniel or Derrynane pier you can hire a boat to take you on a memorable trip to Skellig Michael. The sea journey, sometimes rough, is a good physical pause to allow mental adjustment for a scene that is so very special. Your trip is a pilgrimage to a place of solitude and learning, where western civilisation hung on by its fingernails after the collapse of the Roman Empire. The German film director, Werner Hertzog, captured some of its character in the closing scenes of his film _Heart of Glass_. Weather permitting, you land at Blind Man's Cove amid the squawking of gannets, puffins, fulmars and guillemots, from whom locals used to collect feathers in times past. Up hundreds of steps you rise slowly towards the monastery some 185 metres above the sea. The Gaelic name _Sceilig_ means 'splinter of stone' and how appropriate that name seems to be when you reach the monastery chipped into a ledge of stone and made of the same stone itself. Walls of stone tie the settlement to the ledge where six cells and two oratories have stood for fifteen hundred years. The oratories and the medieval St Michael's Church stand separated from the cells with a well and weather cross in the land between them. The fresh water well on this barren rock is a cause for some bewilderment but it is due to a rock fissure which carries rainwater.

The standing stone slab has a double line cross cut into it and beyond it you see the Little Skellig. Two other cross-inscribed slabs can be seen nearby, sticking out from a pile of stones. The monks' graveyard contains further cross slabs, one of which has radial markings and may have been used as a sundial.

Mythology tells us that one of the first invading Celts, Ir, was buried on the Skellig after he died rowing to Ireland from Spain. Other ancient accounts also say that Ir's brother Donn was buried here after dying of a plague as a result of a curse by the _Tuatha Dé Danann_, whom the Celts defeated to gain Ireland. Amhairghin, the brother of Ir and Donn and poet-judge of the Celts declared the Skelligs to be _Teach Duinn_, or 'House of Donn'. The use of St Michael's name by the early Christians also suggests that this rock was once a druidic place of worship, for this saint was often invoked to overcome pagan druidic influence. A similar example is the Celtic complex of menhirs and avenues of stone at Carnac in Brittany where Christians built St Michael's Church on top of the mound.

The Vikings raided the monastery of Skellig in 812 and 823 but in 956 Olaf Trygveson, the son of the king of Norway, was baptised here. On the death of his father he returned to Norway to become

Celtic-type ogham stones were found in New Hampshire and Vermont in the early 1970s by Dr Fell of Harvard.

king. He introduced Christianity to Scandinavia but the Danes and Swedes rebelled and killed him in 1000. His son, also Olaf, later became the national saint of Norway.

Skellig was the centre of a controversy between the Celtic and Roman Christian churches. The Celtic churches declined to follow a seventh-century ruling about the timing of Easter and it was not until the medieval period that the Skelligs concurred. The Augustinians gained control of the Skelligs around this time and promoted pilgrimages. The enclosing stone walls as well as the stone steps and pathways are believed to date from this period. Stations of the Cross were set up which required a pilgrim to perform prayers and some daring acts of climbing, including the kissing of a stone tablet at the end of a five-metre projecting rock. Until the twentieth century it was a local custom to row across from the mainland to the Skellig on 29 September, St Michael's Day, to celebrate mass.

When it is time to leave this place of stone and lichen there is a sense of wonder at the human spirit that built here and endured the seasons and solitude year after year. The poem, Patrick's Breastplate, attributed to St Patrick, who brought Christianity to Ireland in 432, captures some of that enduring spirit:

I arise today
Through the strength of Heaven:
Light of sun,
Radiance of moon,
Splendour of fire,
Speed of lightning,
Swiftness of wind,
Depth of sea,
Stability of earth,
Firmness of rock.
(translated from the Irish by Kuno Meyer)

Breaking the Ring

After a visit to the Skelligs the remaining section of the so-called 'Ring of Kerry' seems tame in comparison. The scenery is still pleasant and at times beautiful but the imagery of Skellig remains. At Killorglin we break with tradition and stay with the coast road to Castlemaine rather than heading for Killarney.

Dingle peninsula

The road from Castlemaine to Anascaul passes the beautiful sandy beach at Inch. Further on we come to Dingle, a harbour village, surrounded by mountains on three sides. As Dingle is so close to the sea it is not surprising to find many fish restaurants here.

What is more surprising is the high standard of cuisine in this small town. Eating out in Ireland is expensive, partly due to government taxes on service and wine. Standards can vary dramatically and while in one place you can have a fine meal, next door charcoal steak, tortured mushrooms and drowned cauliflower

Seamus Heaney, a leading Irish poet, wrote of Gallarus and its monks:
Founded there like heroes in a barrow
They sought themselves in the eye of their king
Under the black weight of their own breathing.
And how he smiled on them as out they came,
The sea a censer, and the grass a flame.

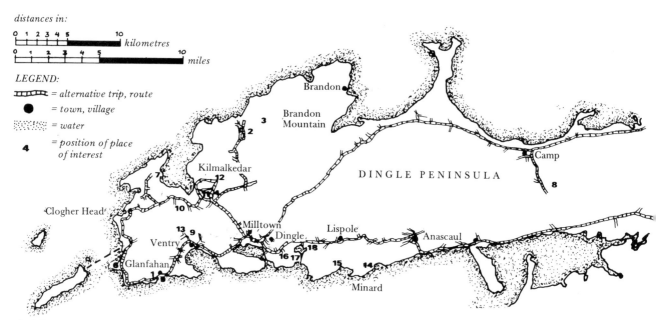

Based on the Ordnance Survey by permission of the Government of the Republic of Ireland (Permit no. 4503).

are on offer for the same price, but not so in Dingle.

The Dingle peninsula is rich in historical remains and Gaelic literary achievement. The Gaelic name for this area, *Corca Dhuibhne*, refers to a group of people who lived here before the Celts, Vikings and Normans arrived. The Gaelic or Irish language is still spoken as the first language by people in the Dunquin and Ballyferriter area.

The Dingle Peninsula Heritage Association has a good exhibition of the local treasures in their museum in Ballyferriter. In a county which can be so money-conscious it is a pleasure to see a group of people coming together to educate locals and visitors about an area that is special in Ireland and Europe.

Dunbeg promontory fort

This fort is the best and most distinctive of those on the Dingle peninsula. It was a defensive settlement for local people and livestock when they were under threat by rival tribal groups. Time of construction could be anytime between 400 BC and 50 BC.

Situated on a finger of land, surrounded by the sea on three sides, the fort could only be approached by crossing several defensive works. The main defensive wall is made up of large stones with a small entrance gate. There is a souterrain leading from the inside of the fort to the entrance where food might have been stored. The outer defensive wall was originally straight but was given its present curved shape during a later reconstruction.

A timber safety fence was erected around the cliff recently and while it may be necessary, its crudeness does detract from the fort.

Similar forts are Dunmore near Coumeenole and Dunanoir near Smerwick village.

The Blasket Islands

Dingle peninsula, the coast near Slea Head

As you round Slea Head the Blasket Islands come into view. The Great Blasket, described as 'a whale with its young' by Sean O'Faolain, produced great Irish literature just before island life collapsed in the 1940s because of emigration and poverty. The Great Blasket has been uninhabited since 1953, but for a period in the late 1920s and early 1930s, the island, whose population never exceeded 200, produced three major writers. Their theme was island life and they were given the encouragement and confidence to write by visiting linguists from Norway, England and mainland Ireland. It was a two-way process with the visitors learning Irish and folklore and the islanders gaining confidence to write about everything including 'a fly buzzing past his ear'.

Today, you can visit the Blaskets from Dingle or Dunquin Harbour. 'Kruger's' pub in Dunquin will tell you the departure times of boats. If you are wondering how the name of a Boer general came to Dunquin it is because a previous owner supported the Boers against the British Empire in Southern Africa and so got the nickname.

The Dunquin pier is reached by a steep zig-zag path and within the fold of the last twist 'black beetles twice as big as a cow', stand upturned and ready for launching. These *naomhógs* or currachs are descendants of the type of leather boat used by Tim Severin in his Brendan Voyage to North America. But visitors generally make the trip to the island in a modern fishing boat. As you sail the sound, sharks may slide past within arm's reach. These dark waters are good for lobsters and mackerel and the Blasket Islanders combined fishing with farming. Sheep and cows were transported by currach across the sound and from island to island and the sea often claimed the lives of the islanders as did sickness and disease. The Great Blasket had no doctor, nurse or priest but an island woman acted as amateur midwife.

When you step ashore having read the 'Blasket Library' (*Twenty Years A-Growing* by Maurice O'Sullivan, *The Islandman* by Tomas O'Crohan and *Peig* by Peig Sayers) you can imagine you feel the weathered hands of the men of oars with rough caps and duller clothes who once stood, hands open, welcoming men such as Robin Flower, George Thompson and Brian Kelly. You pass the village

Dingle peninsula, the tiny harbour of Dunquin. A steep path leads to the pier, where you can admire the fragile currachs, boats that look like giant black beetles when turned upside down.

ruins and beehive hut where all gables face out to sea, and further on the later houses with different orientation, where Peig Sayers once told stories to a packed house.

The beach is below on your left as you look back to the fingers of headland. On Christmas morning the islanders played hurling on this beach in bare feet and so energetic was their game that they were 'destroyed for work for a month afterwards'. Each field you see has its own name but now the rabbits run wild and unchecked destroying the earth walls between fields which were once intensively tilled. Walking to the back of the island you will see dwarf walls where once the local turf was dried.

Blasket Island. I have tried to describe the mind and character of the people I knew so that some memorial of them might remain, for there will never be the like of us again.
from *The Islandman* by Thomas Ó Crohan.

Map of Kerry

LEGEND:

▱▱▱ = *coastal tour*
▱▱▱ = *alternative trip, route*
● = *town, village*
▱▱ = *water*
✳ = *position of place of interest*

distances in:

0 1 2 3 4 5   10 *kilometres*
0 1 2 3 4 5   10 *miles*

County

Mouth of the Shannon

Listowell

Tralee Bay

Ardfert

Fenit   Tralee

Ballyduff   Stradbally

Camp   *Dingle peninsula*

GALLARUS ORATORY

Dingle   Anascaul   Inch   Castlemaine

Ventry

Dunquin   Lispole

Fahan

THE BLASKET ISLANDS

DUNBEG PROMONTORY FORT

Killorglin

Killarney

Dingle Bay

Lough Leane   **MUCKR... HOUSE**

ATLANTIC OCEAN

Ladies View

Cahersiveen   *Iveragh peninsula*

Kenmare

Ballybrack   Sneem

STAIGUE FORT

Caherdaniel

to Glengarriff

THE SKELLIGS   *Kenmare River*

Based on the Ordnance Survey by permission of the Government of the Republic of Ireland (Permit no. 4503).

arbert
ry boat)

Coastal tour county Kerry

Route descriptions correspond with map on opposite page.

Route to Killarney, Tralee
Glengarriff – (N71) Kenmare – Killarney – (N22) Tralee – (Fenit and Ardfert if desired) – (N69) Listowel – Tarbert: Ferry boat to county Clare.

Alternative routes

Iveragh Peninsula
Kenmare – (N70) Sneem – Nedanone: Staigue Fort – Caherdaniel: the Skelligs – Ballybrack – Caherciveen – Killorglin – Castlemaine.

Dingle Peninsula
Castlemaine – (R561) – Inch – Anascaul – (R559) Lispole – Dingle – Milltown – Ventry – Fahan: Dunbeg Promontory Fort – Dunquin: the Blasket Islands – Ballyferriter – Gallarus Oratory – Ballynara – Milltown – Dingle – (R560) Ballyduff – Stradbally – Camp – Tralee.

Further on you come to where paths dip and cross and then rise again, to where the grey light meets the grey stone of the ancient hill fort. It was here that Robin Flower came to sit in solitude and consider his future book, *The Irish Tradition*, an excellent introduction to Irish literature and culture. It is here too that his ashes were brought from England in the late 1940s to mingle with the soil of his adopted island which he loved so much. In his book he recounts a casual meeting he had with an old islander of over eighty years of age who invited him to 'sit down now and we'll have a crack together'. Sitting on the old man's spade, laid crossways over the potato furrows, he listened spellbound to his poetry and prose. 'As I listened, it came to me suddenly that there on the last inhabited piece of European land, looking out to the Atlantic horizon, I was hearing the oldest living tradition in the British Isles.'

This tradition is virtually dead now except for a few isolated pockets in Kerry, Galway and Donegal where the Irish language limps on – the language is becoming like the Great Blasket itself, an uninhabited place of history, culture and beauty.

Gallarus oratory

You will see many beehive stone cells on the Dingle peninsula but Gallarus oratory is unique. The common beehive cell is circular, which suits the corbelling process of building naturally and so is self-suggesting in shape and construction. Gallarus oratory, on the other hand, takes the conscious decision of choosing a special shape and then resolves the structural problems of building that shape.

The rectangular shape of Gallarus is not as inherently stable as the circular beehive when using the corbelling method of construction. However, the builders of Gallarus resolved the problem beautifully by sloping all four walls. The resultant shape has been imagined to represent an upturned boat, a turfstack or a barrow. For nine hundred years, the unmortared stone has kept out the rain. The only missing section of the original building are the crosses which stood at each end of the roof ridge.

Nearby an ancient track, the Saint's Road, leads from the surrounding monastic area to Brandon Mountain and St Brendan the Navigator's shrine. Today, people still wind their way along this path on the last Sunday in June, to kneel where thousands have knelt before them, over the last thousand years.

Chapter 6

Counties Clare and Limerick

The landscape of Clare varies from the high cliffs of Moher in the west, through the limestone fields of the Burren, to the fertile banks of the river Shannon in the east. If you are looking for good traditional Irish music west Clare is the place to go.

Clare has suffered from migration to Dublin and emigration to England and America right up to recent time. Yet Clare helped shape the father of modern Ireland, Éamon de Valera, who was *taoiseach* (prime minister) from 1932 until 1959, except for two short periods. He then became president of Ireland for a further fourteen years. Since de Valera was the only surviving leader of the 1916 rebellion he commanded great influence. After the Civil War which followed independence he formed the *Fianna Fáil* Party and the Irish Press newspaper group. De Valera was the architect of the 1937 constitution and he kept Ireland neutral during the Second World War. To this day, Ireland belongs to no military alliance and has no compulsory military service.

De Valera was a leader of considerable ability but his vision of Ireland is seen as having been too insular and narrow by many of Ireland's youth today. In his national address in 1943 he envisaged an Ireland 'whose countryside would be bright with cosy homesteads, whose fields and villages would be joyous with the sounds of industry, with the rompings of sturdy children, the contests of athletic youths and the laughter of comely maidens, whose firesides would be forums for the wisdom of serene old age'. This quaint vision was dimmed and dulled by huge emigration in the 1950s and it took de Valera's successor as *taoiseach*, Seán Lemass, to get the Irish economy moving and reverse a hundred years of population decline.

Edna O'Brien, the novelist from Scarrif, county Clare, was one of those 'comely maidens' who grew up in the 1940s and early 1950s and rejected the insular vision of de Valera. Her early novels, *The Country Girls, Girl with Green Eyes* and the later *A Pagan Place*, tell of her adolesence, sexual awakening, emigration and loss of religious faith. Her books were banned for a period in the 1960s by a country that felt hurt and betrayed. Now that they are available, changes in Irish society are rendering them historical. Two centuries ago the famous Clare poet, Brian Merriman, explored Irish sexual mores in his classic poem *The Midnight Court*. Edna O'Brien's books are tame in comparison.

Speaking about sexual matters in Ireland is not easy. Older people generally see sexuality within the confines of catholic orthodoxy and many things are left unsaid. Legislation to liberalise the contraception law in 1985 caused political controversy but did succeed; whereas ten years before it had been clearly defeated, when government members, including the *taoiseach*, voted against the measure. Under

Opposite page: The medieval gable of Kilfenora cathedral with the surrounding cemetery, containing some twelfth-century high crosses

Seán O'Casey, playwright and novelist, expressed the frustration of many intellectuals at the parochial, insular views of Irish society under de Valera when he wrote in *The Irish Times* in June 1957: 'Here we have bishops, priests and deacons, a Censorship Board, vigilant librarians, confraternities and sodalities, Duce Maria, Legions of Mary, knights of this Christian order and knights of that one, all surrounding the sinner's free-will in an embattled circle.... The banning of bombs is more to the point than the banning of books, and Christians should know this better than anyone.'

the surface attitudes are changing, the influence of the catholic church is slowly weakening and a more pluralist attitude is gaining ground, but not without strong opposition.

Choice of trips

The coastal tour leads via the Tarbert-Killimer ferry crossing directly from county Kerry to county Clare, a tour which is short but interesting. An alternative choice can be made in Tarbert and provides some impressions of county Limerick as well as Clare. But if you don't want to miss the famous Burren and have enough time, I suggest a combination of both routes – then drive as far as Ennis and link up at Lehinch or Kilfenora.

Miltown Malbay

This small town looks like many other Irish towns but it stands apart as a place for Irish music. West Clare has always been rich in traditional music and since the death in the 1970s of its greatest piper, Willie Clancy, a commemorative summer school takes place annually in Miltown Malbay. The town's population is swollen to over twice its size as Irish and foreign musicians attend classes to learn more about Irish traditional music, instruments and playing techniques. At night the pubs are alive with music, energy and enjoyment.

Even the law is seduced by the music. I overheard an off-duty *garda* (policeman) ask a group of musicians at offical pub closing time; 'Will ye be staying long?' 'Well, that depends on you,' said the musicians, to which the *garda* replied, 'Sure if you are continuing I'll go and get my wife.'

If you are a musician or a visitor interested in another culture's music then the Willie Clancy Summer School is a must for you. It is a delight to see Irish music strong and self confident, in stark contrast to the Irish language which seems destined to become a school language, learnt but unspoken.

The Burren

The Burren area of Clare is a desert of limestone in stark contrast to the green fields you expect to see in Ireland. The grey fields are divided by grey walls, but like any desert, the Burren has its oases. Alpine and arctic plants and flora grow side by side with Mediterranean species in the rock crevices. The warm, damp winds from the Atlantic compensate for the lack of ground moisture. May and June see these plants in full bloom.

Unlike the rest of Ireland, where limestone rock is below the soil's surface, it is completely exposed in the Burren area (the Irish name *Boireann* means a stony rocky place). Geologically, it is 'karstified', with bare limestone pavements with wide joints (called clints and grikes), sink holes, caves and underground streams. Traces of

The exposed limestone area of the Burren, with its many rock crevices and fissures, which in early summer contain rare plants like spring gentians, rock roses and Irish orchids

A grotto of the virgin Mary, near Kilfenora

carbonic acid in the rainfall and decaying organic matter cause
erosion in the limestone which gives rise to unusual rock shapes and
beautifully sculptured caves.

Turloughs (Irish *tuar loch* meaning dry lake) appear after heavy
rain but disappear in a few days. The 160 square kilometres of the
Burren has only one surface river, since most go underground on
route to the sea.

This unique area contains the remains of four centuries of history,
including dolmens, burial chambers, stone forts, castles and
churches. The route chosen from Kilfenora to Ballyvaghan will give
you a representative selection of the Burren's well-preserved past. If
you have the time and the interest in this area then you might like to
complete the circuit from Kilfenora to Newtown Castle and return to
Kilfenora via Poulnabrone Dolmen and Leamaneh Castle.

Kilfenora

This small village has been well endowed by history and contains a
fine series of carved high crosses and a 'cathedral'. Through the
efforts of local people, the Burren Display Centre was set up in
Kilfenora to promote an appreciation of this unusual area. I visited
the centre with my husband and after we had paid our entrance fee
we were asked to wait ten minutes until the next tour began. We
viewed the usual collection of arts and crafts and at the stroke of three
o'clock were called upon to join the tour by a clear and resolute
voice. We found ourselves alone with our young girl guide whose
voice projection was more suited to touring bus groups. Without
tonal deviation she delivered her knowledgeable lecture with

Head sculpture of a clergyman in the
Burren Display Centre

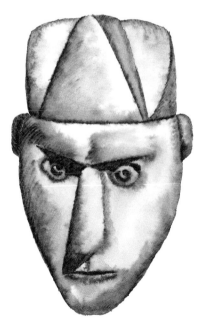

shoulders back and direct eye contact. We lacerated our lips with teeth marks in attempts to control a fit of the giggles and were only released from our agony when we offered no questions. It would have been unforgivable for us to laugh because her heart was in the right place, even if her voice was not.

Close to the display centre is a group of interesting high crosses, of which the Doorty cross is the most detailed, with symbolic carvings open to many interpretations. Part of the cathedral, with its stepped medieval gable, still endures as a place of worship surrounded by its crosses.

Caher Ballykinvarga

Some two kilometres from Kilfenora is the double walled stone fort of Ballykinvarga. You will have to walk a few hundred metres before you see the Iron Age fort surrounded by its *chevaux de frise* limestone pillars. The term *chevaux de frise* is derived from a military expression used to describe how Dutch Frisians used spikes to impede attacking cavalry. There are only a few remaining examples of this type of fort defence in Europe, found mainly in Spain and Portugal. Ireland has three other such forts, of which two of the most impressive are found on the Aran Islands.

The curious straight joints in the outside walls are believed to be sectional construction joints to allow workers access to the inside of the fort during construction. The very thick walls have two internal terraces and the view from the top of the wall, across the *chevaux de frise*, must have been a comforting sight for the ancient fort defenders.

Some seven kilometres further north is another ring fort called Cahermacnaghter which was occupied until the eighteenth century. It is of smaller diameter than Ballykinvarga, measuring some thirty-two metres. It is entered via a medieval two-storey gateway, and foundations of rectangular buildings of a similar date can be seen inside the old stone walls.

A newly painted cottage in Askeaton: the cat is sitting in front of the door and to the left are the ruins of what was probably the old house/stable, now almost completely overgrown.

These later buildings were used by the O'Davoren family where they taught the Gaelic Brehon Law in their famous medieval law school. Irish Brehon Law was formally abolished in 1606 at a ceremony in Ennis Friary and replaced by English Common Law, which deprived Irish women of the right to their own property, a right they enjoyed under the Brehon Law. The new English law also meant that royal succession was through the eldest male child rather than by clan selection as under the Gaelic system.

Newtown Castle

Enjoy the drive and view from Corkscrew Hill to Newtown Castle. The sixteenth-century, five-storey defensive tower is of unusual shape with a circular tower set upon a square, pyramid-type base. This shape of base acts as a buttress and the interaction of geometrics, of round upon square, gives rise to 'shot holes' at the base of the round part of the castle on all four sides. The domed first- and third-storey ceilings still retain the outline of the wickerwork which held the wet mortar in place during construction.

Aillwee Cave

It is hard to distinguish the Aillwee Cave Centre from the surrounding landscape because of its sensitive architectural design. The centre offers organised tours and safe access to part of the three-hundred-metre-deep cave.

The cave is the remains of an underground river caused by melting snow during the Ice Age. The first main chamber is called Bear Haven because of the bear 'beds' found there. Other chambers have limestone cascades, stalactites, stalagmites, straws, curtains and rimstone pools before the tour ends at the edge of an underground river. Bring your jacket with you because the depth of the cave means that there is a constant temperature of ten or eleven degrees centigrade throughout the year.

Clare has many other caves but they are only suitable for experienced potholers. Pollnagollum cave has eleven kilometres of surveyed passages and at Ballnablacken a stalactite of more than seven metres in length is the longest in western Europe.

Alternative route via county Limerick

Askeaton

The road from Tarbert to Askeaton gives extensive views of the tidal Shannon estuary as you enter county Limerick. Askeaton Castle, built in the fifteenth century, stands where a twelfth-century Norman castle once stood. It is an extensive but badly damaged ruin, entered via a farmyard full of chickens and dogs.

The Franciscan friary dates from the same period but is in a far better state of preservation. A well-preserved cloister seems too small

Ballyvaghan, Newtown Castle, a circular tower set upon a square base

in relation to its surrounding buildings. The carved windows, the sedilia and the triple tomb niches are worth a look.

Great chases and shrieks of laughter can be seen and heard as local children run around the tops of the walls. In the fading evening light a little tinker (gypsy or traveller) boy asks for his photograph to be taken. He stands rock-solid to compensate for the slow shutter speed, with hands firmly locked in a religious manner. After the click the hand opens out and asks for ten pence. An outcast has to live on his wits and take his chances, but when I declined to pay he ran off, well used to such answers.

Adare

This is a neat and picturesque village of thatched cottages, tree lined streets and medieval monuments. The best of the monastic ruins is the fifteenth-century Franciscan Friary situated in the middle of a golf course in the grounds of Adare Manor. The Manor itself is a Gothic revival mansion built in 1832 and within its grounds it contains two other monuments, Myra Church and Desmond Castle. The latter was built on a former ring fort in the early thirteenth century and was the scene of many battles. The Desmond name is derived from a corruption of the Irish *Diese Munt*, meaning south Munster, the geographical area this family controlled for so long.

On the east side of the village near the bridge is the fourteenth-century Augustinian friary. It is now used as a Church of Ireland church and school. It is one of the few existing churches that can give us a reasonable idea of how Irish medieval churches originally looked. The skill and ability of the stonemasons can still be admired today.

Limerick city

This city dates from the mid-ninth century and witnessed siege and destruction in the late seventeenth century.

Today, it is a city of grid iron streets grafted onto the older curving street pattern near the river crossing, which made Limerick so important strategically. It is a city starting to redevelop as new industries are set up in that region. New cultural activities, such as the Belltable Arts Centre, are slowly adding a new dimension to this industrial city.

The Limerick novelist, Kate O'Brien, described her home town as wearing 'the grave, grey look of commerce', and that is still the dominant feeling today. Limerick has its monuments and 'places of interest', a list of which the tourist office will give you.

Limerick has a traditional reputation for religious observances such as 'retreats' and 'novenas'. A retreat usually consists of a number of days of special prayer, contemplation and a series of lectures by the priests of the Redemptorist order. In one boys' school a Redemptorist priest dressed in his black cloak with a silver heart gave such a vivid and dramatic 'sex and sin' lecture that he received spontaneous applause from the impressed pupils, much to his own embarrassment.

Schools in Ireland are generally segregated into religiously controlled boys' and girls' schools. Girls' schools in particular often require their students to wear a school uniform and support that requirement with the argument that it is an egalitarian measure. Whatever the reason, these crude uniforms certainly cannot enhance or encourage self-confidence in body-conscious teenagers. Most

This reconstruction of an ancient Irish lake dwelling, or crannog, can be seen in Craggaunowen, near Quin

primary and secondary schools, except state community and vocational schools, are under religious management control despite the fact that they are state funded and have very few religious priests or brothers as active teachers. With religious vocations dropping and secular demands rising, changes must come with time – 'Irish time' no doubt.

Bunratty Castle and Folk Park

There are so many roofless ruins in Ireland that it is a pleasure to see an expertly restored fifteenth-century castle such as Bunratty. Originally restored in the 1960s by state architects it is now run as a non-profit enterprise. Revenue in excess of expenses is spent in improving the castle and folk park.

A good history and guide to the castle rooms is provided at the entrance. The genuine fourteenth- to seventeenth-century furniture and furnishings add a further interesting dimension to an already special castle. In the evening two medieval-type banquets are held in the main dining hall.

Outside in the castle grounds, a folk park consists of a number of typical farmhouses and village buildings from the nineteenth century. As in most folk parks you see the picturesque without the squalor, the ideal without the compromise, yet it is still interesting to see and visit.

Coastal tour counties Clare & Limerick

Route descriptions correspond with map on opposite page.

Route to the Burren
(N69) Tarbert – ferryboat to Killimer – (N67) Kilrush – (R483) Cooraclare – Greegh – (N67) Miltown Malbay – Lehinch – Ennistimon – (R476) Kilfenora: the Burren Display Centre and cathedral – Caher Ballykinvarga stone fort – Cahermacnaghter stone fort – (N67) direction Ballyvaghan: Newtown Castle (or via R480 along many monuments to Ballyvaghan) – Aillwee Cave – (N67) Burren – Gort, county Galway.

alternative route via county Limerick
Tarbert (N69) – Glin – Foynes – Askeaton: castle & friary – Kilcornan – Adare: friary – (N20) Limerick city – (N18) Bunratty: castle & folk park – Hurlers Cross – (R471) Sixmilebridge – (R462) Kilmurry – (R469) Quin: Craggaunowen project – Ennis – (N18) Crusheen – Gort, county Galway.

Craggaunowen near Quin

The Craggaunowen development is another type of folk park in that it contains a modern reconstruction of a Bronze Age lake dwelling, or crannog, and ringfort in the grounds of a restored sixteenth-century tower house.

A crannog is an ancient Irish lake dwelling built by an isolated farming family for protection. The word *crannóg* derives from the Irish word *crann*, meaning a tree, as a large amount of timber was used in its construction. Log platforms or clay mounds were enclosed by timber stakes and reinforced with layers of loose stones, peat and brushwood, sometimes even animal bones. A timber palisade and/or wickerwork perimeter wall was usual. Wickerwork was also often used on the floor of houses within the palisade. Mud and wattle walls and a thatched roof were the common hut building materials.

The Craggaunowen crannog has a causeway linking it to the mainland but boats, made from hollowed-out trees, were the more common way of coming and going. The dampness of the crannog has helped to preserve many objects of archaeological interest. Evidence of the smelting of iron and bronze for weapons and tools has been found in excavated crannogs.

The reconstructed ringfort at Craggaunowen is an enclosed circular space surrounded by an earth bank and fosse or ditch. The fosse was dug out and the material used to make the raised bank, which is planted with a defensive timber palisade. Ireland contains over thirty thousand ringforts, compared to some two hundred *crannógs*. The Craggaunowen reconstructions give a reasonable conjectural view of what these ancient dwelling places were like, based on archaeological research.

The sixteenth-century tower house contains medieval art objects. Nearby, Tim Severin's 'Brendan Voyage'* boat is on display in a misconceived, glasshouse-type structure. The boat is made of leather hides stitched together over a delicate timber frame and its design is based on the ancestor of Irish boats called currachs or *naomhógs*. While the boat seems out of place with the other exhibits, you can only but admire the effort, ingenuity and courage of Tim Severin as described in his book on that eventful journey.

Kilrush

mouth of the Shannon

* See page 70

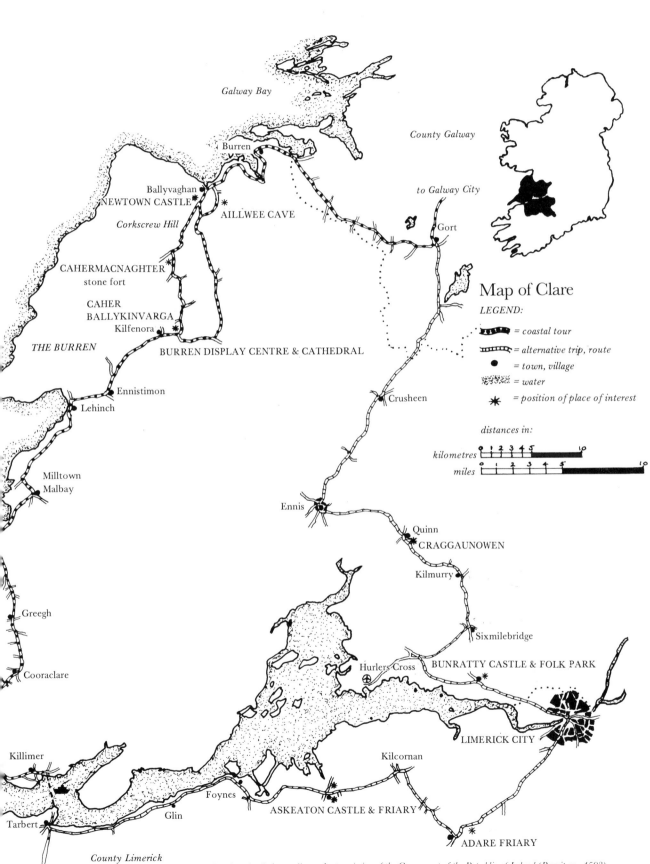

Galway Bay

County Galway

Burren

to Galway City

Ballyvaghan
NEWTOWN CASTLE

Corkscrew Hill

AILLWEE CAVE

Gort

CAHERMACNAGHTER
stone fort

CAHER
BALLYKINVARGA

Kilfenora

THE BURREN

BURREN DISPLAY CENTRE & CATHEDRAL

Map of Clare

LEGEND:

= coastal tour

= alternative trip, route

● = town, village

= water

✳ = position of place of interest

distances in:

kilometres

miles

Crusheen

Ennistimon

Lehinch

Ennis

Quinn
CRAGGAUNOWEN

Milltown
Malbay

Kilmurry

Greegh

Sixmilebridge

Cooraclare

Hurlers Cross

BUNRATTY CASTLE & FOLK PARK

LIMERICK CITY

Killimer

Kilcornan

Foynes

Glin

ASKEATON CASTLE & FRIARY

Tarbert

ADARE FRIARY

County Limerick

Based on the Ordnance Survey by permission of the Government of the Republic of Ireland (Permit no. 4503).

If you had been on the quay at Rossda-
lough that night after Nora had gone,
you would have seen an old man in a
fishing boat. He had a pot of tar beside
him and he was obliterating the name of
the boat. He could do that, but he was
unable to efface the name from his heart.
He had named the boat after his daughter.
(translated from Pádraic Ó Conaire's
Irish story 'Nora Mharcais Bhig')

Chapter 7

County Galway

The two distinct parts of county Galway – the east with its
limestone pastureland and the west with its scenic mountains – are
separated by Lough Corrib, and Galway city mediates between the
two. W.B. Yeats came to spend his summers in the genteel east,
while J.M. Synge went to the more robust westerly Aran Islands.
Padraic Pearse came to the 'real Ireland' of Irish-speaking
Connemara to write his poems and plan the 1916 revolution. Liam
O'Flaherty left his native Aran to write and help start the tiny
Communist Party of Ireland. Virginia Woolf found the locals 'more
amusing than any London society' and the countryside 'lovely but
very melancholy'.

Galway is still a place of amusing talk but less and less of it is in

the Irish language. In Ireland three per cent of the population speak Irish as their first language, yet over eighty per cent think it is important that their children should learn it at school. As happens so often in Ireland, there is a huge gap between intention and action, between what is said and what is done. The Irish language began to decline when the Irish lost the Battle of Kinsale in 1601 and Ireland's political leaders fled the country. The language began to crumble without a Gaelic political and social order to support it. In the late eighteenth century, Irish became identified with poverty, illiteracy and national failure. Under the National School system from 1831 until 1904, no Irish was taught in schools. All business of state was conducted in English only. The Famine of 1845-48 was most severe in the poor Irish-speaking areas. A million died or emigrated, and emigration or migration from Irish speaking areas has continued ever since.

Spurred on by Padraic Pearse's prophecy that 'if Irish were to be lost Ireland would perish', written just before he was executed for leading the 1916 revolution, the Irish government has tried to revive

In cabin
and fields, they still
speak the old tongue.
You may greet no one.
To grow
a second tongue, as
harsh a humiliation
as twice to be born.
Decades later
that child's grandchild's
speech stumbles over lost syllables of an old
order.
'A Grafted Tongue' by John Montague

These traditional Irish boats, called currachs, are made of a delicate timber frame which is covered with tarred canvas. (Note that the oars don't have flat end-pieces.) Because of their lightness and flexibility they are still used for fishing.

the language. It has tried to create employment in Irish-speaking areas, but there are signs that even in these heartlands the language is slipping away under the pressure of tourism, television and the departure of their youth.

Travellers

The tinkers or travellers are a group of people on the fringes of Irish society. You will have seen their caravans and encampments on the roadsides and encountered them begging, especially in Dublin. Traditionally they were associated with Galway, which gave us the word 'rahoonery' to describe the forceful eviction of travellers from settled communities. The men deal occasionally in cars, carpets and electrical goods while the women are responsible for the daily income through begging.

Sharon Gmelch, who lived with travellers for a year and wrote *Tinkers and Travellers, Ireland's Nomads,* tells us that the best 'begging costume' is a blanket and a baby accompanied by the words 'Can you give a little help, and God bless you.' Begging is a serious business and large sums of money are aften collected. Excessive drinking and illiteracy are major traveller problems and they find it hard to 'pass' or settle in Irish society. Tradition says that they have their origins in evictions by landlords from property in the west of Ireland in the eighteenth and nineteenth centuries, and got their original name, tinkers, because they were travelling tinsmiths.

Government efforts at resettlement have been outstripped by the growing numbers of travellers, a result of huge families. Also, the sites offered are unattractive. Resistance from the settled community to housing travellers in their areas has been, and continues to be, a major problem.

Thoor Ballylee, near Gort

The poet W.B. Yeats bought this sixteenth-century tower house in 1916 and used it as his summer residence for thirteen years. It first came to his notice during his many visits to Lady Gregory at nearby Coole Park. In his poem 'My House' he wrote of Thoor Ballylee:

An ancient bridge, and a more ancient tower,
A farmhouse that is sheltered by its wall,
An acre of stony ground
Where the symbolic rose can break in flower.

Yeats's poetry certainly continued to flower and the surrounding area is frequently featured in his writings. He was drawn to this place by its past associations with Gaelic kings, Norman invaders and stories about a local witch. A poem of restoration and dedication is carved on the tower's wall for all to read. At the end of that poem he prophesies the tower's ruin once again, but luckily further restoration in the 1950s saved the building. It is open to the public and you can climb 'The Winding Stair' and see much the same view Yeats described. A rare collection of first editions is on display and a sound guide to the tower and grounds is available in different languages.

Who is your God? And where is he?
Is it in the skies he is, or in the earth,
or under the earth, or upon the earth,
or in the seas, or in the streams?
Is he young? Is he beautiful?
Has he sons and daughters?
Is he one of the everliving ones?
from Lady Gregory's *Book of Saints and Wonders*

Thoor Ballylee, near Gort, the tower house from the sixteenth century which was used as a summer residence by the poet W. B. Yeats

Coole Park, a short distance from Thoor Ballylee, is a landmark for Irish literature. It was here that Yeats and Lady Gregory conceived the Abbey Theatre. It was here that the major figures of the Irish literary revival came as guests and were obliged to carve their initials on the copper beech 'autograph tree'. And it was here that Lady Gregory learnt Irish and translated old Celtic sagas.

Yeats had a great affection for Coole Park and for Lady Gregory, and he wrote in 'Coole Park 1929', three years before she died:

Here traveller, scholar, poet, take your stand
When all those rooms and passages are gone,
When nettles wave upon a shapeless mound
And saplings root among the broken stone,
And dedicate – eyes bent upon the ground,
Back turned upon the brightness of the sun
And all the sensuality of the shade –
A moment's memory to that laurelled head.

The house did disappear except for stump walls and the estate now belongs to the state Forest and Wildlife Service, who have planted new saplings, but not 'among the broken stone'. The pool of 'The Wild Swans at Coole' is still here and maybe even swans, although I did not see any when I visited.

The economic and physical scars left by the bitter and bloody Civil War tarnished the 'terrible beauty' of newborn independence and the poetic vision that went with it. In 1931 Yeats looked back and wrote of 'Coole Park and Ballylee':

We were the last romantics – chose for theme
Traditional sanctity and loveliness;
Whatever's written in what poets name
The book of the people; whatever most can bless
The mind of man or elevate a rhyme;
But all is changed, that high horse riderless,
Though mounted in that saddle Homer rode
Where the swan drifts upon a darkening flood.

Galway city

Galway city is a place more of atmosphere and social activity than of beauty. Music, song and drink are pursued with ability, full voice and dedication. During the week of the Galway Races – an important event in the horse-racing calendar – the city seems to stop work and indulge itself in complete entertainment. Poteen (illegal 'whiskey') can be had if you ask the right man at the right time. Time stands still, or appears to, especially if you drink too much poteen. Mary O'Neill wrote of Galway:

I know a town tormented by the sea
And there time goes slow
That the people see it flow
And watch it drowsily.

Galway owes its importance as a town to the sea and the Spanish ships that came here with wine and gold in times long past. That past is celebrated in Eamon O'Doherty's sculpture of steel sails in Eyre Square based on the shape of the famous red-sailed Galway 'hookers' or fishing boats. The remainder of Erye Square is dedicated as a memorial to the assassinated American president, J.F. Kennedy, but in design terms, it is neither an urban square nor a small-town fair green. In a way, this unresolved ambiguity, this oscillation between being a town and a city is what makes Galway outrank other places of larger population such as Limerick. The university, the neighbouring Irish-speaking areas and tourism give status, culture and money to a town that easily accommodates all three.

Status came early to Galway when it was settled in the thirteenth century by fourteen Anglo-Norman families called the 'Tribes of Galway'. For four hundred years these families held all civic powers and tried their hardest to anglicise Galway. They passed laws which declared 'that neither O or Mac shall strutte ne swagger thro the streets of Galway'. Such law did not keep the O'Flahertys of Aughnanure Castle, near Oughterard, from regulary raiding the walled town. Over the west gate an inscription reads: 'From the fury of the O'Flahertys, good Lord deliver us'. The ruling Galway families also passed laws restricting the wearing of bright clothes and silk by men as well as colourful hats by ladies. They even tried to restrict the drinking of whiskey. Needless to say, their efforts have left no impression on present day natives.

The one impression the tribes did leave is the sorry story of the Lynch hanging. In 1493 the son of Lynch, the mayor-cum-magistrate, killed a Spanish guest for showing interest in his girlfriend. He was tried and sentenced to death by his father. No local would act as hangman and, afraid that powerful family friends might free the condemned young man, Lynch took his son from the prison next to his house and hanged him from the upstairs window. In a twist of irony, this incident gave rise to the expressions 'Lynch law' and 'Lynch mob' to describe a crowd taking the law into their own hands, outside of the official law courts. The upstairs window of the Lynch house is in Market Street but there is some doubt as to whether it is authentic, since the house style dates from the sixteenth and seventeenth centuries.

The Galway Spanish connection is fondly remembered and locals claim that Christopher Columbus stopped by for mass on his way to discover America and 'that fact accounts for a Galway man in his crew'. The ill-fated Spanish Armada was wrecked off the Galway coast in 1511 and the survivors came ashore and settled in Galway. A tiny segment of the old town walls, situated close to the river and port, is called Spanish Arch. Nearby is the city museum.

Spain still seems to influence Galway building styles if you are to judge by the sight of crude modern bungalows with 'Spanish arches' out past the seaside suburb of Salthill. The elected local authority has been criticised for over-ruling its own planners and permitting rampant housing development along the coast which had previously been refused. The visual arts of planning and design are still not appreciated in many parts of Ireland today, although great importance is attached to literature, as Ireland's very high level of book purchase confirms.

From the promenade at Salthill, where 'the breakers pour themselves into themselves', you can see the Aran Islands floating out of the sea. Behind the Spanish Arch you will find the ferry boat and fellow-visitors with Nikon, Zeiss and Kodak cameras in search of the 'real Ireland' of Irish-speaking Aran.

These waterpumps are common in the west of Ireland and most of them are still working perfectly

Alternative route

Aran Islands

If you have read Synge or O'Flaherty or have seen the 1930s film _Man of Aran_ then today's Aran may disappoint you. Tourism has come to the islands, for the better from the point of view of the island's economy, for the worse from the cultural point of view. The largest island, Inishmore (great island), is the one you can reach direct from Galway and it is the most tourist conscious of the islands. Inisheer (east island) and especially Inishmaan (middle island) are more isolated – you can reach them by small locally owned vessels from Inishmore and there is also a ferry service between Inisheer and the Clare coast – and so are also more traditional. You will be spoken to in English unless of course you too can speak Irish and the islanders will offer bicycles and jaunting cars for rent on Inishmore. A bicycle is a good way to get around but do keep an eye out for the bumps that can unsaddle the unsuspecting.

Once you have accepted that time stands still only in museums then you will enjoy your visit to these remarkable islands, and realise that in comparison to the Greek islands, they are virtually untouched by exploitation. The locals do have a very strong sense of pride and I heard one Galway city women declare 'They [the Aran islanders] think they are more Irish than the rest of us.' In the pub, later that night, an Irish-speaking man from county Roscommon was chided by islanders for not being 'a real Irishman'. The Roscommon man retorted that they, the islanders, were half descended from Cromwellian troops garrisoned on the island in the seventeenth century. This remark caused uproar and a torrent of abuse.

The landscape of the Aran Islands is closely related to the Burren area of county Clare and its exposed limestone pavement. Rainfall disappears through the porous limestone soon after falling. After a dry period of a few weeks, water becomes scarce and sanitary facilities can become primitive. Simple rain troughs have been constructed to conserve water but they are not sufficient for prolonged periods without rain. You may have noticed, when you were approaching the islands, the series of terraces stepping their way across the land like a huge stairs. These steps are due to the erosion of the layers of limestone and shale that make up the local rock structure.

The huge force of the Atlantic ocean beats remorselessly against the southern and south-western side of the islands creating sheer cliffs not unlike the Cliffs of Moher. In winter storms, sea boulders are often hurled over the clifftops by the power of the breakers and the resultant collections of boulders are called storm beaches. Due to the severity of the winter all housing is on the more sheltered, north-eastern side of the islands. Here sand beaches replace sheer cliffs. An Trá Mór (the big strand) at the eastern end of Inishmore is becoming a lagoon.

Elsewhere, early Christian churches have been covered by shifting sand dunes. On Inisheer, Teampall Chaomháin, the Church of Saint Cavan, is threatened with shifting sand, but due to religious devotion to him the locals clear out the sand from the stone ruin on

Summer and solstice as the seasons turn,
Anchor our boat in a perfect standstill,
The harbour wall of Inishmore astern
Where the Atlantic waters overspill -
I shall name this the point of no return...
from 'Leaving Inishmore' by Michael Longley

the saint's feast day in mid-June each year.

There are seven stone forts on the islands, four on Inishmore, two on Inishmaan and one on Inisheer, all believed to date from the early Celtic period some two to three thousand years ago. Mythology and island folklore claim the forts were built by the *Fir Bolg* (Bolg Men) after they were defeated by the magical *Tuatha Dé Danann* (The Peoples of the Goddess Dana) on the mainland of Ireland, at the battle of Mag Tuirid. The *Tuatha Dé Danann* were later ousted by the Celts. Some historians claim the forts belonged to a people making a last stand against their enemies and point to Dún Aengus on Inishmore, with its cliff edge site, as proof of that theory. However, the majority of the other six forts do not have similar cliff locations and no fort had a well or water supply, which meant that they could not withstand a siege. It is more probable that the forts belonged to politically strong and wealthy farmers who had the time, surplus wealth, organisation and manpower to build these impressive buildings. Generally speaking, the best land surrounds the forts.

The unique cliff location of Dún Aengus on Inishmore gives it a special quality. The four-metre-thick walls are six metres high and were constructed by building up two separate walls and then filling in

Dún Chonchúir (Conor), Inishmaan, one of the seven stone forts on the Aran Islands

between them with rubble material. The buttresses to the inner wall date from the time of restoration in the 1890s. Like the stone fort at Caher Ballykinvarga in Clare, Dún Aengus has a *chevaux de frise*. So too has Dún Dubhchathair (sometimes called Duchathair or Doocaher), a promontory fort less than two kilometres south-east of Dún Aengus. All the forts have an atmosphere of power but I thought Dún Chonchúir on Inishmaan could rival the more highly thought of Dún Aengus in majesty.

The remnants of the old Gaelic *clachán* or farm cluster can still be seen today. This is an irregular grouping of houses and farm buildings without a street or square which originally had no public buildings such as shops or pubs. An 'infield' and 'outfield' in common ownership provided crop and grazing land respectively. Now most land is in private ownership. Seaweed and kelp production still continues as a local industry and these products are used for land reclamation.

Scholars came here to learn Irish and discover the old Gaelic way of life at the end of the nineteenth century, as they came to the Blasket Islands off the Kerry coast. Encouraged by W.B. Yeats 'to express a life that has never found expression', John Millington Synge came to the islands each summer from 1898 to 1902. Here he found inspiration for his plays *Riders to the Sea* and *The Playboy of the Western World*. The plot for the latter developed from an island story about a Mayo man who sought refuge there after killing his father in a fit of rage. So distraught and remorseful was he that the islanders hid him for months from the hated police until he made his way to America. Locals say that he was hidden in a wall cavity of Dún Chonchúir. Synge wrote of the islanders' attitude that 'if a man has killed his father and is already sick and broken with remorse, they can see no reason why he should be dragged away and killed by the law.'

Small fishermen's shed near Ballyna-hinch, in beautiful Connemara

Liam O'Flaherty was born the year before Synge first came to these islands. A man of courage and forthright socialist views, he wrote of the hard island life in his stories, 'Famine', 'The Landing', and 'Going into Exile'. Emigration was a fact of life but emigration of young men and women to America in the nineteenth century was seen by parents as a form of death since the emigrants were unlikely ever to return. An 'American wake' was held the night before leaving. Liam O'Flaherty writes of a grieving parent: 'My children, oh, my children, far over the sea you will be carried from me, your mother' and she began to rock herself and she threw her apron over her head.'

For me, leaving was harder than coming, taking more than memories and drawings, for we had come forewarned but left disarmed. Like Parisians, proud and chauvinistic, the Aran Islanders have something besides tourism and television that other people have not.

Aughnanure Castle near Oughterard

On the road to Oughterard, 'gateway to Connemara', gateway to holiday homes with Mercedes and Volvos outside, where the landscape is 'rugged but not too wild', you will find Aughnanure Castle, the stronghold of the ferocious O'Flahertys. From here they launched their attacks on Galway town until their castle was first destroyed by English forces in 1572, some seventy years after it was built. The O'Flahertys regained their castle for a period in the sixteen hundreds when part of their clan recognised the crown of England, but that century of war with Cromwell and William of Orange saw the O'Flahertys expelled again.

The six-storey castle tower has two defensive bawns still to be seen, but the large banqueting hall collapsed long ago into an underground river, now diverted. The inner defensive wall has a beautiful mosque-like dovecot at one corner, made-up of corbelled* stone. The castle tower roof has been reconstructed in an authentic historical manner. From the parapet you have a good view over Lough Corrib where our guide of many stories told us that he rowed across in good weather for a pint of stout on the other side. 'Only one pint?' I asked in disbelief. 'Well, a bird never flew on one wing,' came the answer. When I enquired could I sketch him, his blue eyes lit up in his broad Galway face. He took off his cap, smoothed his grey hair, turned down his curling shirt collar, placed his hands behind his back like an officer standing at ease and said, 'You know, this is no ordinary castle, it was featured on an Irish twenty-two pence postage stamp.'

The guide of Aughnanure Castle, Thomas Walsh

Alternative route

Connemara

This is wild landscape, beautiful in the sun, brooding in drizzle, depressing in the rain. So if the sun shines, or even if it is interrupted by heavy showers, it is a place to roam around and enjoy. You don't

* See page 15

have to stick to any proposed route but follow your heart's desire, for there is beauty to match your expectations in every valley. Mountains give way to fields which give way to bog which gives way again to rivers and lakes.

Clifden is the major town of Connemara and the scene of the annual Connemara Pony Show. Letterfrack has a national park worth a visit, even if its rival in Glenveagh in county Donegal has more to offer. The National Park employs the only known civil service sheepdog to keep sheep out of the park, much to the annoyance of the local farmers. It seems the offending sheep are 'accidentally on purpose' let into the park, for a free graze.

Kylemore Abbey, a former castle, is now run as an expensive international girls' school by the Benedictine nuns from Ypres. The friendly sisters welcome visitors to their extensive grounds and building. A small Gothic church, past the main house, commemorates the wife of the original builder Mitchell Henry, who died near here in a horse accident.

The drive into Leenane, or Leenan, skirts the side of Ireland's only genuine fjord, Killary Harbour, where oysters are grown in special floating cages.

Journey across to Maam, or Maum, Bridge and on to Clonbur and Cong if you have the time. Keane's pub at Maam Bridge is a former Bianconi horse coach station with an open fire and a piano. An old bachelor with a friendly heart told me he was looking for a lady with R and D. Before my mind could wonder on possible permutations he gave me his requirements, 'Respect and Decency'. If the ladies of Merrimans' *Midnight Court* got their hands on him they would 'Refute and Debauch' him.

To or from Dublin

In recognition of the fact that many visitors to Ireland travel to Galway from Dublin or vice versa. I have included a few suggestions for places worth visiting along the way. They are Clonfert Cathedral and Portumna Castle in the south of county Galway and Clonmacnois in county Offaly.

Clonfert Cathedral

At first glance this cathedral looks more like a lichen-covered parish church set within a graveyard. But have a closer look at the entrance portal and note the columned arcade with carved human heads. Above the arcade, set within recessed triangles, are rows of alternating marigolds and human heads. Although dating from the Romanesque twelfth century, when heads were a feature of decoration, this particular design seems very influenced by the more primitive Celtic motif of *têtes coupées* or severed heads. The remainder of the church dates from the fifteenth century.

Detail of entrance portal, Clonfert cathedral

Clonmacnois, a former monastic city, was founded by St Ciarán around 545. It is situated south of Athlone, on the river Shannon in county Offaly.

I and Pangur Bán my cat,
'Tis a like task we are at:
Hunting mice is his delight,
Hunting words I sit all night.
ninth-century poem in margin of manuscript by unknown scribe

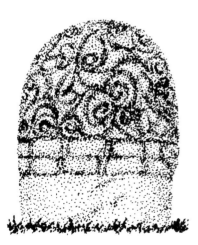

The Turoe stone near Loughrea

Clonmacnois

This former university of Christian learning dates from the middle of the sixth century and was famous throughout Europe for a long period. It is situated on Ireland's largest river, and so was easily accessible when the country was densely forested. Unfortunately for the monks and scholars the Vikings found it an easy and worthwhile place to raid.

It is famous as a burial place for saints and kings and the names of individual churches recall their original patrons. Great books were lovingly compiled and transcribed by scholars such as Maol Muire, who commenced the famous 'Book of the Dun Cow' in the early twelfth century. This book relates the pagan Celtic epic saga of the *Táin Bó Cuailgne.* Strange as this may seem, it was an attempt by the early Irish church to accommodate the Celtic spirit of the people and show itself as the natural inheritor of that tradition. The Celtic ornamented grave slabs and high crosses bear witness to the success of that strategy.

In 1179 Norman invaders burnt over one hundred houses within the walls of Clonmacnois and the university went into decline. The final blow was struck when the English garrison of Athlone plundered the site and removed all valuables in 1552, thus ending a thousand years of learning. A brochure is available locally giving detailed information on individual buildings.

Or do Mhíchíl: 'A prayer for Michael', cross slab in Clonmacnois, county Offaly

Journey to Portumna Castle

On route to Portumna you pass through Loughrea town whose catholic cathedral has an interesting selection of twentieth-century stained glass windows by Evie Hone and Michael Healy.

North of Loughrea, near the village of Bullaun, stands the Turoe Stone. It is compared with the similarly shaped and decorated Omphalos stone in Delphi which was seen as the navel or centre of the world by the ancient Greeks. The Celts raided Delphi in 290 BC and the Turoe Stone dates from the same period. Much discussion revolves around its possible ritual and phallic connotations. It was moved to its present position from a ring fort called Rath of Fearmore or Rath of the Big Man.

Portumna Castle dates from 1618 and has a well-proportioned, first-floor Renaissance doorway. The corners of the castle have square towers and it is presently undergoing restoration. A period knot garden is envisaged and the castle may become a school for craftsmen.

Based on the Ordnance Survey by permission of the Government of the Republic of Ireland (Permit no. 4503).

Coastal tour county Galway

Route descriptions correspond with map.

Route to Galway city
(N18) Gort: Thoor Ballylee castle – Ardrahan – Oranmore – (N6) Galway city. From Galway harbour the ferry boat leaves for the Aran Islands (*alternative 1*).

Route to Oughterard, Leenane
Galway city – (N59) – Moycullen – Rosscahill – Aughnanure Castle near Oughterard – Maam Cross – *alternative 2*: Connemara – (N59) Recess – Clifden – Letterfrack: national park – Leenane.

Route to county Mayo
Maam cross – (R336) – Maum – Leenane – (N59) direction Westport, county Mayo.

To (or from) Dublin
Via Clonfert and Clonmacnois:
Galway city – (N6) Oranmore – (R348) Athenry – Kiltullagh – Cloonymorris – Ballinasloe – (N6) Garbally – (R355) Laurencetown – Clonfert: cathedral – back to Ballinasloe – (R357) Shannonbridge – Clonmacnois monastic site – Ballinahowen – (N62, N6) Moate – Kilbeggan – Kinnegad – (N4) Maynooth – Dublin.
Via Portumna:
Galway city – (N6) Oranmore – (N6) Loughrea: cathedral – (R350) the Turoe Stone – (N65) Portumna: castle – (R489) Birr – (N52) Tullamore – Kilbeggan – (N6) Kinnegad – (N4) Maynooth – Dublin.

County Roscommon

Map of Galway

LEGEND:

= coastal tour
= alternative trip, route
● = town, village
= water
✳ = position of place of interest

distances in:

kilometres

miles

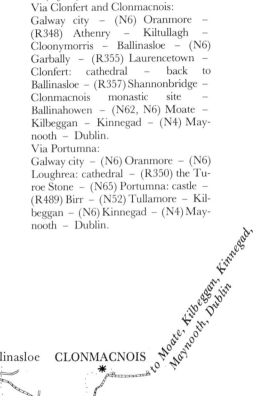

Ballinasloe   CLONMACNOIS

to Moate, Kilbeggan, Kinnegad, Maynooth, Dublin

Athenry   Cloonymorris

nmore

Shannonbridge

Kiltullagh   ✳ **THE TUROE STONE**

CLONFERT CATHEDRAL

Laurencetown

LOUGHREA CATHEDRAL

Lough Rea

County Offaly

Ardrahan

to Tullamore, Kilbeggan, Kinnegad, Maynooth, Dublin

PORTUMNA CASTLE

Birr

Gort ✳**THOOR BALLYLEE CASTLE**

rren

to Ennis

Lough Derg

Chapter 8

County Mayo

This is the forgotten tourist county, not for want of beauty but rather because of visitor laziness. Heinrich Böll, the German writer, spent family holidays here in the mid-1950s. He wrote in his *Irisches Tagebuch* or *Irish Journal* of a country on the threshold of change, where old patterns still held sway. In his epilogue, written years later, he writes: 'we had caught Ireland at that historic moment when it was just beginning to leap over a century and a half and catch up with another five'. Killala, in north Mayo, has the huge Japanese Asahi chemical textile plant as proof of that leap.

Industry now accounts for one-third of total Irish employment, while agriculture amounts to one-fifth, which is the reverse of the situation when Böll wrote his diary. The IDA (Industrial Development Authority) provides a package of financial incentives and special tax concessions to native and foreign industrial enterprises. Many of the foreign backed industries, like Asahi, are export-orientated. Some of them have been known to close down when their parent company has been reorganised in their own country or when their grants and tax concessions have expired. Dependence on foreign investment is still strong but the realisation that they are not all reliable is forcing a rethink of past policies.

The year 1879 put Mayo on the political and religious map with the founding of the Land League and the apparition at Knock. The Land League, founded by Mayoman Michael Davitt, publicised the gross injustices of the landlord system. The following year saw two thousand evictions until the peasant farmers of Mayo made their stand against Captain Boycott. The British government was forced to settle and a number of land bills enabled tenant farmers to buy the land they tilled. The result today is the almost religious attachment many Irish country people have to the land for which their forefathers struggled, no matter how poor the soil may be.

The apparition at Knock and the village's subsequent development as a place for international pilgrimage sponsored particularly by its dynamic parish priest wed religious devotion with economic development. The holy mountain of Croagh Patrick, where pilgrims often walk in slanting struggle against mountain wind and rain, represents a more demanding form of devotion.

The physical beauty of Mayo is found along its rugged coastline of headlands and islands, the conscious hand of design in Westport town and house, and the tenacity of places and their people from Ballintubber to Achill Island.

Croagh Patrick

This is the cone-shaped holy mountain of Ireland where St Patrick spent the forty days of lent in 441. Tradition says that during that time he extracted a promise from God that Ireland would never lose

Opposite page: A graveyard near the village of Dugort on Achill Island in a drenching downpour

When Holy Patrick, full of grace,
suffered on Croagh that blest place,
In grief and gloom enduring then
For Éire's women, Éire's men.
(translated from the twelfth century
Dinnshenchas 'History of Places')

'The Faith'. If you come here on the last Sunday in July you will also witness that faith.

The cloud tents the mountain and the sprinkle of rain blesses the meandering march of pilgrims, some treading in bare feet, stick in hand, prayers on lips, past stones that could speak of devotion over centuries. Climbing seven hundred metres closer to their God they come to stand and kneel in formal prayer, their exertions misting their plastic raincoats. Frothing whispers become a communal prayer as drizzle transforms to rain and later, still praying, the pilgrims flow like rivulets down to where they began, renewed.

Westport

Ten kilometres from Croagh Patrick you come to Westport, one of the few designed towns in Ireland. Its architect, James Wyatt, made the most of his site. The Carrowbeg river is walled and tree-lined to give the North and South Mall an urban rather than a parochial feeling. The river bubbles over weirs, its peaty water the colour of Coca Cola. The northwestern end of the Mall is connected by James Street to the Octagon containing the Market House and Town Hall. In its centre stands a limestone Doric pillar, centre of visual gravity and focus of axes of three streets. At the top of Shop Street an awkward concrete clocktower replaces an earlier waterpump and poorly imitates the axis role of the Doric column. The junction of the Octagon with its three streets is well handled with transition from straight street to octagon accomplished with elegance. The only intruder is a business to the right of the Town Hall which was reconstructed with a crude flat roof, ugly windows and scaleless shopfront.

If you leave the Octagon by Quay Street you will come to the house of the gentry who built Westport. Situated in a beautiful man-made setting of trees, river and ponds, Westport House has an austere facade. Originally designed by Richard Castle in 1731 it was extended and enlarged by Thomas Ivory and James Wyatt later that century. The house sits on the foundations of an earlier O'Malley castle of which the dungeons still remain. They have been commercially 'horrified' to extract money and squeals from children while their parents wander through the house. The parents don't escape the torture of being lured by arts and crafts, jewellery, swords and antique guns as they make their way around house and gardens. I was told that the strong commercial presence was necessary to save the house from 'crippling taxes'.

The house has a fine entrance hall with barrelled ceiling and a centrally placed Sicilian marble stairs which stand where originally there was an open courtyard. The diningroom is well proportioned with interesting plasterwork. The writer William Thackeray likened the view of island-scattered Clew Bay, to 'so many dolphins and whales basking there'. The terraces and balustrades leading down to the water's edge date from 1913, where once the sea lapped at the old castle walls.

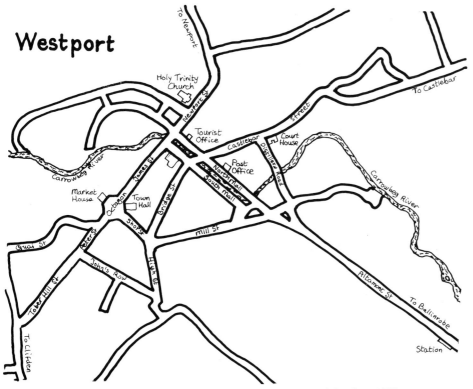

Based on the Ordnance Survey by permission of the Government of the Republic of Ireland (Permit no. 4503).

Alternative routes

Ballintubber Abbey

The Westport to Ballinrobe road is sometimes narrow and often bumpy. You turn off at Killavaly for Ballintubber along dry-stone walls and new houses with sunset patterned gables. The abbey awaits visitors as it has always done since 1216, when it first opened its doors to pilgrims on their way to Croagh Patrick. The ancient pilgrimage path, *Tóchar Phádraig,* to the holy mountain can still be traced today.

Originally the abbey was set in a lakeside clearing surrounded by dense forest. The Irish name for county Mayo means the 'plain of the yew trees', but the yews are long since gone. The lake is also gone, or more exactly it has receded, due to land drainage schemes. A hollowed out tree canoe was found in one of the surrounding fields and archaeological research indicates an ancient landing slip nearby.

Push hard to open the heavy timber door into this beautifully restored church. The stone slab floor slopes from the west door towards the altar and heightens your feeling of procession towards the chancel. The narrow windows are splayed to let the light spill and wash the rough white walls from which the oak roof springs. The north and south transepts have niches for a devotional altar, fifteenth- and sixteenth-century tomb slabs and a baptistery with a thirteenth-century font. Sunlight bursts through the four east windows of warm, red and yellow stained glass and I thought of the roofless ruin that people worshipped in for two centuries. Cromwellian troops burnt

Nineteenth-century poem by the blind Mayo poet Raifteirí:
I am Raifteirí, the poet, full of courage and love,
my eyes without light, in calmness serene,
taking my way by the light of my heart,
feeble and tired to the end of my road:
look at me now, my face towards Balla,
performing music to empty pockets!
(translated from the Irish by Thomas Kinsella)

and tried to demolish this abbey in 1653, but the people kept faith and never abandoned their church. Finally restored in 1966, for its seven hundred and fiftieth anniversary, it lays claim to uninterrupted church attendance for all that period, despite war, supression and proscription.

Outside of the church are the remains of a cloister, chapter house and calefactory. The tapering flagstones of the cloister walk mark graves from the thirteenth and fourteenth centuries. The supporting pillars of the cloister arcade are all sculptured differently – Irish individualism of course – some have masons' marks. The calefactory or warming room was heated by under-floor air ducts to and from the fireplace and the restored floor indicates the system used.

Knock

On the 21 August 1879, an apparition of the Blessed Virgin Mary, St Joseph and St John appeared on the southern gable of the village church at Knock.

Knock is to Croagh Patrick as brass is to gold. Whereas the mountain is a place of ancient and devout pilgrimage, the village of Knock is a more recent place of religious excursion and, like Lourdes and Fatima, it has become a tourist venue as well as a place of pilgrimage. Over three-quarters of a million people visit annually. The tiny village of a few hundred people now has a basilica capable of holding twenty thousand pilgrims. Unfortunately, the basilica does not respond to the occasion and is lacking in architectural merit, as is the crude glass extension covering the gable of apparition.

Across the road from the old church and new basilica is a 'village'

A mason's mark on one of the differently sculptured pillars of the cloister arcade of Ballintubber Abbey

of souvenir shops, more than I ever saw in the St Peter's Square area of Rome. Shops with names such as St Brendan or St Martin all sell the same crude souvenirs. Nearby the Knock Marriage Bureau helps put people in contact with prospective partners, while its small neighbouring building houses a folk museum.

In the village of Knock a number of 'restaurants' provide snacks and meals for visitors. One of them served us black tea, mouldy bread and dry cake for twice the price you would pay in Westport for better quality. The youthful waitresses in this barn of a tea-house were so young that they ought still to be playing with their dolls and tea-sets, rather than fumbling in the greasy till of exploitation.

Achill

The road from Newport to Mulranny passes a landscape full of little lakes, rugged hills with dry stone walls and fuchsia hedges; and a seascape of countless little islands. Cows graze the 'long acre' (roadside), and if you are lucky they will slowly move aside; otherwise you will have to be patient.

You will also have to be patient with the weather. On consecutive days I witnessed Achill in drenching downpour and sunny splendour. Heinrich Böll described it in a philosophical way: 'The rain here is absolute, magnificent and frightening. To call this rain bad weather is as inappropriate as to call scorching sunshine fine weather.' The combination of wind and rain causes even the sheep to huddle in a hollow of the blanket bog, tangled and windswept. It is impossible to go outside in this type of weather so find a nice place with good company and enjoy yourself. Once the rain clears there is much to see.

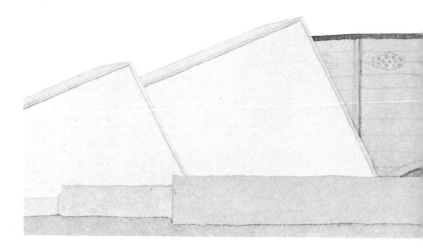

The name Achill derives from the Irish *acaill* meaning eagle. Sea and golden eagles were plentiful here until the nineteenth century. The people are hard workers but their efforts bring little from a reluctant land. But their attachment to 'their' land is such that few leave it completely. It was a common pattern for these farmers to work their autumn, winter and spring in Britain as seasonal farm or construction workers and return home for the summer. These migrant or emigrant workers are even brought home to be buried. While I was there a group of Achill people were going to Shannon Airport to collect and escort home the coffin of a fellow islander, who had died after living over forty years in New York.

The huge basilica in the tiny village of Knock, the Lourdes of Ireland

Cross slab with shamrock decorations in Straid Abbey on the main Castlebar-Ballina road

In her story, 'The Lost Child', Mary Lavin tells of finding half-concealed flat grave-slabs belonging to unbaptised infants along 'the tufty shore-grass' of Dugort Strand. The sand is almost orange in colour although it is called 'Golden Strand' on the signpost. The picturesque village of Dugort has a contentious history. In the early nineteenth century a protestant missionary settlement established itself on mountain land at Dugort. It attempted to convert local catholics through both religious and physical example. Land was reclaimed for farming and the present village of Dugort established. The mission acquired title to three-fifths of Achill within a short period and tension with local catholics reached a climax during the Famine of the 1840s when it is alleged that relief food was only supplied to those islanders who would become protestants. The derogatory name 'soupers' was given to those who received food or soup because they changed their religion. Financial difficulties forced the mission to close its schools and abandon Dugort in the late nineteenth century. However, it did leave its mark by way of the tourist industry it helped to establish by founding Achill's first hotel in Dugort.

Nearby on the south-facing lower slopes of Slievemore is a deserted village of some one hundred buildings. All that remains are the stone walls now covered in moss and lichens. All other signs of human endeavour have been gnawed away by wind, rain and sun. The stone gables have little niches for pots and kitchen equipment. No one is sure why and when this place was deserted, maybe because of the Famine or landlord evictions. Not far away megalithic tombs mark where a far earlier people ceased to live and were buried under similar but larger grey stone slabs.

It is striking to see flat-roofed houses around Achill which seem so impractical in this wet winter area. Near Keel, a convent with a more conventional roof catches my attention. It is painted Virgin Mary blue, so blue against the so green background that it looks like a painting by Magritte.

Further on the road brings you to Dooagh village and Keem Strand. North-west of the strand, on the lower mountain slopes is Bunowla 'booley village'. The word booley derives from the Irish word *buaile,* meaning a milking place, and refers to the seasonal moving of livestock practised by local farmers until the end of the nineteenth century. The circular stone walls were roofed with grass sods and were the temporary homes of herdsmen and their families during the summer months when they brought their livestock to fresh upland grazing.

Take the 'Atlantic Drive' on your way back and enjoy the raw landscape. At Kildavnet, just past Cloghmore, is the sixteenth-century tower castle of the pirate queen Grace O'Malley. She ruled the seas of Mayo and was invited to visit Queen Elizabeth I because she had pillaged ships of the Spanish Armada. Her son helped the English to blockade the later Spanish expedition to Kinsale in 1601. He was knighted and later made Viscount of Mayo, but in 1629 he was killed by his brother in law and buried in a specially carved tomb in Ballintubber Abbey. A similar O'Malley castle can be found on Clare Island in Clew Bay.

To Sligo

Driving north from Mulranny via Bangor to Ballina you pass places that will delight sea and river anglers alike. The skill of the fly fisherman holds sway here. The river Moy and Lough Conn are good for trout and salmon. The landscape changes from wild Atlantic to small fields whose hedges crouch away from the wind. Seldom do you hear the gargle of tractors in these fields. Valley sheep, smeared with their owner's mark, are the only real sign of human presence.

A white-haired man in a dark house looks out as I sketch his beautifully constructed turf stack. Outside his old man's long underwear, rain-wet and sodden, drips from a sagging clothesline between rusting, sloping poles. The black and white sheepdog followed the old man to his gate. 'Don't be put off by the look of me,' he said, 'I gave up looking in mirrors long ago.' And he told me that once the saints rang their monastery bells, long before the bad years came and the potato crops died and Boycott fled and the Irish language too. I thanked him for our talk in the low lingering light and in parting he advised 'Remember, in Ireland you can't keep a secret among three people, unless two of them are dead.' I said I would remember and I hope he doesn't mind me telling you our conversation.

Small cottage on the Corraun peninsula
on the way to Achill Island

Coastal tour county Mayo
Route descriptions correspond with map.

Route to Westport and county Sligo
Leenane (N59) – Westport: house and town – *alternative 1*: (R335) Croagh Patrick – *alternative 2*: (R330) Killavally – (N84) direction Ballinrobe: Ballintubber Abbey – Ballyglass – Claremorris – (N17) Knock. (From here you can link up with Charlestown.)

To Sligo
Westport – (N60) Castlebar – (N5) Bellavary – Swinford – Charlestown – (N17) Tobercurry, county Sligo.

alternative 3: Achill Island and Sligo
Westport – (N59) Newport – Mallaranny (Mulranny) – (R319) Achill Sound – Keel – Dooagh – Dugort – Bunacurry – Dooego – Cloghmore: Kildavnet Castle – Achill Sound – Corraun – Dooghbeg – Mallaranny (Mulranny) – (N59) Ballycroy – Bangor – Crossmolina – Ballina – (R297) Kilglass, county Sligo.

Killala Bay

County Sligo

ahybaun

Crossmolina
Ballina

to Sligo town

Tobercurry

Lough Conn

RANGE

Lough Cullin

Charlestown

Swinford

County Roscommon

Bellavary

wport

ESTPORT
Castlebar

KNOCK

BALLINTUBBER
ABBEY

Killavally

Map of Mayo

Ballyglass
Claremorris

Lough Carra

LEGEND:
= coastal tour
= alternative trip, route
= town, village
= water
= position of place of interest

Lough Mask

distances in:
kilometres
miles

Based on the Ordnance Survey by permission of the Government of the Republic of Ireland (Permit no. 4503).

Chapter 9
County Sligo

This county of flat-topped mountains, picturesque lakes and sand-dune beaches belongs culturally to the poet W.B. Yeats and spiritually to two famous women, Medb and Markievicz, one a queen-goddess, the other an aristocrat-revolutionary.

Although separated by two thousand years, Queen Medb and Countess Constance Markievicz are of special importance to the history and development of Irish women. Medb, or Meave as she is sometimes called, is a powerful figure in Celtic legend. She freely interchanges between queen and goddess in many ancient sagas and is the maker and consort of kings. In the famous saga, the *Táin Bó Cuailgne* (The Cattle Raid of Cooley), Medb leads a huge army from the western province of Connacht to the east coast in search of the best bull in Ireland. This story is the first real glimpse we get of women in ancient Ireland. Other sources tell us that Celtic women often fought alongside their men: in the seventh century a law was passed which fined men who employed women in battle. Until the Norman and Elizabethan conquests of the twelfth and sixteenth centuries Irish women had extensive rights in the areas of marriage, divorce and inheritance. English Common Law and church reform relegated women to a subservient position.

In the late nineteenth and early twentieth centuries women such as Lady Gregory of Coole Park in Galway and Constance Markievicz (née Gore-Booth) of Lissadell in Sligo come to the fore in cultural and political activities, respectively. Yeats knew both women and wrote of them in his poems. He also drew upon Queen Medb, the Celtic archetypal queen-goddess figure of the ancient sagas. By doing so, he helped to rekindle a national pride and spirit, which had been almost crushed by political failures and the Great Famine of the 1840s. This period of exploration of ancient roots became known as the 'Celtic Twilight' or 'Literary Revival'. In a play by Yeats from that period called *Cathleen ni Hoolihan*, the poet draws upon the famous ninth-century poem, 'The Old Woman of Beare', as a point of reference for the new Ireland he envisaged.

Peter: Did you see an old woman going down the road?
Patrick: I did not: but I saw a young girl, and she had the walk of a queen.

Today, Irish women are following the developments of the women's movement in western Europe and America without their excesses (exclusiveness) and in a more cautious manner. Arlen House, a small but very worthwhile women's press, publishes books by women writers and there are now women's centres and feminist groups in many Irish towns. In politics, and particularly in government, however, women are still few and far between.

The Old Woman of Beare

The sea crawls from the shore
Leaving there
The despicable weed,
A corpse's hair.
In me,
The desolate withdrawing sea.

The Old Woman of Beare am I
Who once was beautiful
Now all I know is how to die
I'll do it well.

Look at my skin
Stretched tight on the bone.
Where kings have pressed their lips,
The pain, the pain.

I don't hate the men
Who swore the truth was in their lies.
One thing alone I hate –
Women's eyes.

The young sun
Gives its youth to everyone,
Touching everything with gold.
In me, the cold.

The cold, Yet still a seed
Burns there.
Women love only money now.
But when
I loved, I loved
Young men.

Young men whose horses galloped
On many an open plain
Beating lightning from the ground
I loved such men.

And still the sea
Rears and plunges into me,
Shoving, rolling through my head
Images of the drifting dead.

Ancient sites and stories of Sligo

The hill country of county Sligo has been free from agricultural encroachment since prehistoric times and as a result there is a fine collection of ancient graveyards. Besides Carrowmore near Medb's grave, there is the excellent court cairn at Creevykeel, just beyond the village of Cliffony, on the Sligo to Donegal road. Going in the opposite direction, from Sligo to Boyle, I found the passage graves of Carrowkeel and its neighbouring 'village' of fifty beehive huts most impressive. Set on a hilltop of the Bricklieve mountains overlooking Lough Arrow, between Castle Baldwin and Ballinafad, it is reached by an untarred mountain road. It has cruciform and multiple-cell type passage graves. The cruciform type have narrow passages and were roofed with large lintels while the larger chambers were usually roofed in a dome form using the corbelling* method. In the multiple-cell type, the passage is divided into segments with the main chamber separated from the adjoining cells by 'septal stones' or sills.

The *Lebor Gabala* (the Book of Invasions) relates the mythological Second Battle of Magh Tuiredh, between the Fomoire and the *Tuatha Dé Danann*, not far from Carrowkeel. The Fomoire (meaning 'under-demons') were defeated when their leader Balor was killed by a sling shot from Lug. To ensure their harvest the Celts adopted Lug as one of their gods and celebrated his festival, *Lugnasad* in August. The modern Irish word for August, *Lúnasa* is derived from his name.

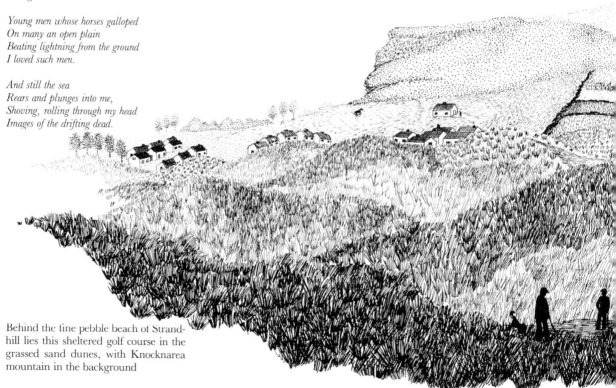

Behind the fine pebble beach of Strandhill lies this sheltered golf course in the grassed sand dunes, with Knocknarea mountain in the background

* See page 15

Sligo town

This town is the centre of the Yeats 'industry'. An international summer school is devoted to the writer every year for a fortnight in August. The members' festival club has a late-night drinking licence, much to the envy of the locals. But not being a member proved no obstacle to my local assistant who through soft talk and a final gallop up the stairs when the doorman was distracted, gained us a long night's journey into drink. As a result, I cannot be held responsible for any omissions in my town tour the next day.

The town is surrounded on three sides by mountains and hills. The name Sligo is a corruption of its Irish name, which means 'the shelly river'. A recently constructed promenade along this river, the Garvoge, would be more pleasant if the neglected rears of the houses were improved. Nevertheless, Sligo has a pleasant air to it and its public buildings, such as the town hall and courthouse, have a sense of occasion and grandeur beyond what you normally find in a town of its size. The streets still retain a unified visual structure and some fine Edwardian shop and pub fronts.

If you are parking a car, then the car park off Wine Street is the place to go, as Sligo suffers from traffic jams and it is difficult to find a parking spot on the street. Unfortunately, the neighbouring supermarket development is a design disaster.

Near the junction of Wine Street and Union Street, you will see a fine half-slated house with pleasant details. If you continue along Lord Edward Street towards the railway station you may see what looks like grafitti on number twenty-one. In fact, it is the writing of

A soldier cries
Pitifully about his plight;
A king fades
Into the shivering night.

Does not every season prove
That the acorn hits the ground?
Have I not known enough of love
To know it's lost as soon as found?

I drank my fill of wine with kings,
Their eyes fixed on my hair.
Now among the stinking hags
I chew the cud of prayer.

Time was the sea
Brought kings as slaves to me.
Now I near the face of God
And the crab crawls through my blood.

I loved the wine
That thrilled me to my fingertips;
Now the mean wind
Stitches salt into my lips.

The coward sea
Slouches away from me.
Fear brings back the tide
That made me stretch at the side
Of him who'd take me briefly for his bride.

The sea grows smaller, smaller now.
Farther, farther it goes
Leaving me here where the foam dries
On the deserted land,
Dry as my shrunken thighs,
As the tongue that presses my lips,
As the veins that break through my hands.

translated from the Irish by Brendan Kennelly

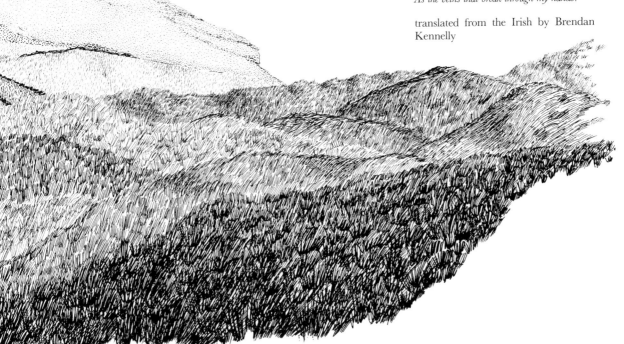

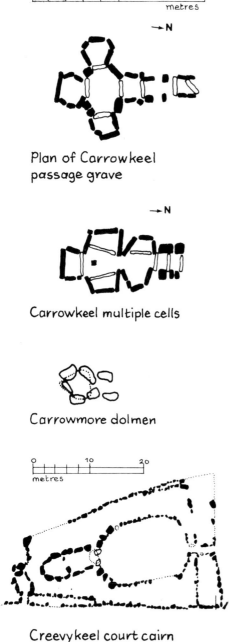

Plan of Carrowkeel
passage grave

Carrowkeel multiple cells

Carrowmore dolmen

Creevykeel court cairn

From: *Antiquities of the Irish
Countryside* by Seán P. Ó Ríordáin

Plans of ancient graveyards in county
Sligo

its elderly owner, Mrs Curran, whose condemnation of local habits is read with interest. Another town character is a Trotsky look-alike, who is Ireland's only self-professed communist town councillor.

Back towards the river and along Stephen Street you will find the County Museum and Municipal Art Gallery. The museum has an exhibition of archaeological and local historical interest and, of course, a special section on W.B. Yeats, including his Nobel Prize medal. The art gallery next door has a good collection of paintings by Jack B. Yeats, brother of the poet. Having such a famous brother has overshadowed the artistic achievements of Jack Yeats. His earlier water-colours of proud Connemara peasants are almost in an heroic, political poster style; while his later oil paintings are more impressionist in temperament. His work and that of other Irish artists exhibited in the gallery are worth visiting. The Yeats Building at Hyde Bridge acts as a gallery for visiting exhibitions, lectures and workshops.

Lough Gill is close to the town and you can of course take a boat trip to W.B. Yeats' Isle of Innisfree. Other organised trips include a conducted walking tour of the town lasting one and a half hours. The tourist office will give you details. Sligo has a good selection of different types of music, so just ask what's on tonight.

Strandhill

On the road out to Strandhill you will see Coney Island, whose name means rabbit island. The New York island of the same name is supposed to have been named by a Sligo sailor who saw that it too was full of rabbits.

Strandhill village is no more than a loose clustering of buildings close to a well-known beach resort. On sunny weekends the beach is crowded with visitors. During high tides and with the right wind conditions, good surfing rollers add extra variety. Walking along the shore you will find some fine beach pebbles, many with interesting fossil remains. But the most interesting aspect of Strandhill is the huge sand dunes south-west of the sea-front car park. They become larger and more magnificient the further you walk. Even on a windy day you will find a sheltered nook to watch the wind toss and turn the long dune grass. The uninteresting non-fossil remains of human tossing and turning was noticed by a Dutch friend who commented, 'Just like Holland twenty years ago.'

Looking across the golf course you see Knocknarea mountain with its nipple-like cairn, 'where passionate Maeve is stoney still'. The old Irish name of *Miosgán Meadhbha* suggests that this ten-metre-high by sixty-metre-wide mound of stones is the burial place of the legendary Queen Medb of Connacht. The mound is thought to cover a passage grave and was probably built by neolithic peoples around five thousand years ago. From the top of the stone pile you get a panoramic and windy view of Sligo Bay and the Donegal and Mayo mountains. Some four hundred metres north-east of where you stand, you will find remains of several small circular enclosures. Archaeological excavations revealed arrowheads, flint and pottery from 2300 BC.

Five kilometres by road south-east of this place is Carrowmore megalithic cemetery. Excavation unearthed large deposits of sea-shells, indicating that sea-food was an important part of the diet of these people. The excavated burial chambers had cremated remains dating from 3300 BC. Since the nineteenth century over one hundred passage graves and dolmens have been destroyed and only forty now remain in this, the largest megalithic graveyard in Ireland.

Drumcliffe graveyard

This must be one of the most visited graveyards because W.B. Yeats is buried here. The grave looks icy clean but his epitaph is more chilling:

Under bare Benbulben's head
In Drumcliffe churchyard Yeats is laid
An ancestor was rector there
Long years ago, a church stands near,
By the road an ancient cross
No marble, no conventional phrase;
On limestone quarried near the spot
By his command these words are cut:
Cast a cold eye
On life, on death.
Horseman, pass by!

Yeats's 'ancient cross' dates from around AD 1000 on the site of a former monastery of St Colmcille. It shows Adam and Eve, Cain killing Abel and Daniel in the lions' den as well as some skilful Celtic ornaments. Tradition says that the remainder of the lightning-damaged round tower will fall on the wisest man who passes it, but if Yeats could have passed we have nothing to worry about.

Nearby, the same St Colmcille was involved in a battle over the ownership of a copy of a manuscript he had made. The king had decreed: 'To every cow its calf, and to every book its copy'. But Colmcille had fought against that judgement and in remorse left Ireland for Scotland where he promised to save more souls than had been killed in battle. Copyright dispute, seventh-century style.

Lissadell

Just past Drumcliffe you turn off for Lissadell House. Yeats used to visit the beautiful Gore-Booth sisters, Eva and Constance, in their home here, which is now open to the public on weekday afternoons.

The Irish name for Lissadell means 'blind man's fort', and refers to a thirteenth-century poet who lived in the area, called O'Daly. According to the medieval Annals of the Four Masters a tax collector was sent to O'Daly by the local chieftain O'Donnell in 1213, but the poet felt himself to be above taxes and killed the tax collector after he had insulted him. O'Donnell took to arms and pursued O'Daly to his refuge in Galway, where the poet tried to calm his fury with a poem:

What reason for such wrath can be?
The rascal bandied words with me.
I took an axe and hewed him down –
Small matter for a Prince's frown.

(translated from the Irish by Robin Flower)

The poem did not succeed and O'Daly was chased to Limerick and on to Dublin before making for Scotland. He visited the Holy Land with the fifth crusade but eventually was allowed to return home after writing a series of poems which softened the heart of O'Donnell. He died a blind man at Lissadell fort. It is not known if Yeats knew this story but if he did I'm sure he would have approved of the haughty poet's action.

Lissadell House is late Georgian in style, dating from 1836 and built of local limestone. The room where Yeats stayed is over the porch, while the windows of the bowed rear facade are the 'great windows open to the south' he refers to in his memorial poem to the Gore-Booth sisters:

The light of evening, Lissadell,
Great windows open to the south,
Two girls in silk kimonos, both
Beautiful, one a gazelle.
But a raving autumn shears
Blossom from the summer's wreath;
The older is condemned to death,
Pardoned, drags out lonely years
Conspiring among the ignorant.
I know not what the younger dreams –
Some vague Utopia – and she seems,
When withered old and skeleton-gaunt,
An image of such politics.
Many a time I think to seek
One or the other out and speak
Of that old Georgian mansion, mix
Pictures of the mind, recall
That table and the talk of youth,
Two girls in silk kimonos, both
Beautiful, one a gazelle.

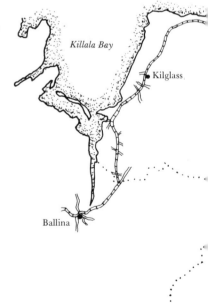

Coastal tour county Sligo

Route descriptions correspond with map on opposite page.

Route to Sligo town and Lissadell
From Kilglass (R297) – Dromore West – Templeboy – Ballysadare; or from Tobercurry – (N17) Ballynacarrow – Collooney – Ballysadare – (N4) Bally-drenid – Strandhill: Queen Maeve's grave and Carrowmore megalithic cemetery – Sligo town – (N15) Drumcliffe: high cross, round tower and Yeats's grave – Lissadell: house – Cliffony: Creeveykeel court cairn – Bundoran – county Donegal.

These two sisters belonged to the landed gentry of the nineteenth century, but Eva became a poet and Constance a suffragette and republican revolutionary. Constance Markievicz was a commander in the 1916 uprising but was spared execution because she was a woman. In the general election of 1918 she was elected as the first woman to the British parliament and later became minister of labour in the first Irish government. Sean O'Casey, the playwright and labour activist, disliked her and in his autobiographical books he states that she was forever playing with a revolver and chatting about 'the workers'. Whether Yeats's or O'Casey's view is true does not really matter now, but we should be grateful that the house still stands as a memorial to Irish literature and women, unlike Lady Gregory's Coole House, of which little remains.

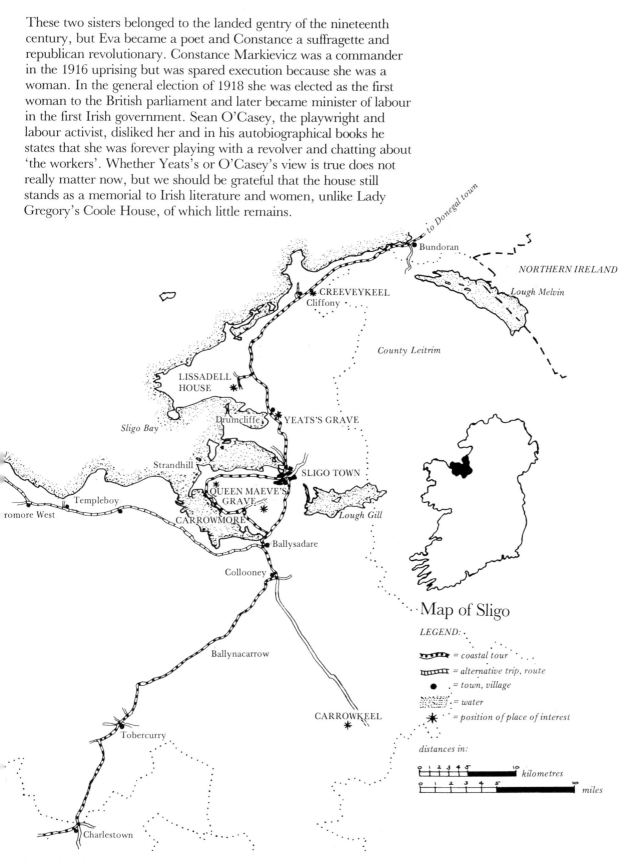

Map of Sligo

LEGEND:

〰〰〰 = coastal tour
〰〰〰 = alternative trip, route
● = town, village
░░░ = water
✳ = position of place of interest

distances in:

kilometres

miles

Based on the Ordnance Survey by permission of the Government of the Republic of Ireland (Permit no. 4503).

Chapter 10

County Donegal

This county is sometimes referred to as the Alaska of the Republic of Ireland, since it is virtually cut off from the rest of the republic by the border with Northern Ireland. In fact Donegal is the most northerly county in Ireland, though politically it is part of the 'South'. That same border segregates Derry city from its natural Donegal hinterland to the detriment of both places.

Church by Liam McCormick in Burt, inspired by the _Grianán_ of Aileach stone fort nearby

Historically Donegal was divided into east and west by its mountains and the Irish language continued to be spoken in the less colonised western areas. Now roads cross these beautiful mountains and valleys of few houses and many rivers. When you meet someone on the road, do return their salute; a raised index finger from the steering wheel will do nicely. With the bumps, twists and poor signposting on some of these roads, you will need to keep your two hands firmly on the steering wheel.

And if, as happened to us, your car decides to take a rest, I hope you are as fortunate as we were. No sooner were we looking at the engine, than the first Donegal car stopped to offer assistance. Further on we came upon what appeared to be a traffic jam in the middle of a lonesome glen. In fact it was a funeral procession. Bonnet to bumper, the cars follow with even speed a neighbour and friend on his last journey down the road to where the priest and altar-boys wait. Neighbours and friends shuffle on leftover confetti in the long evening light, coffin on shoulders, past marble pillars, to the waiting trestles and the smell of incense. Thomas Kinsella grasped this moment of primeval clash and clang:

> Sanctus. _We listen with bowed heads to the clash of chains_
> _Measuring the silence. The pot gasps in its smoke._
> _An animal of metal, dragging itself and breathing..._

And then neighbours and friends follow in single file along the aisle to where the family stands exchanging handclasps and hugs. Outside handshakes return hellos – 'I haven't seen you in ages.' 'Isn't it a fine turnout, the biggest in a long time?' 'Sure hadn't he [the deceased] a long innings and a good life right to the end?' An old woman, unsettled by the occasion, sought comfort from her pregnant daughter. Behind her but beside me, handshake and hello spoke lightly and with ease, but not without poignancy. 'If Seamus was here he would say he had made room for those who have yet to come into the world; he was that sort of man.'

Donegal people are hard workers who don't undersell themselves. In times past they worked as migrant harvesters in Scotland where they lived in shanty town type accommodation called 'bothies'. Peadar O'Donnell, revolutionary and writer, captured that Donegal of the early twentieth century in his novels _Islanders_ and _The Knife_. Today, outside Moville, a more famous writer, Brian Friel, is neighbour to the architect Liam McCormick. Like the poet Seamus Heaney, the playwright Friel captures and distills aspects of Ireland's past and present in such plays as _Philadelphia, Here I Come!_ and

Opposite page: Glenveagh National Park in northern Donegal is well worth a visit, because of the exceptional gardens and the imposing landscape. This drawing shows the rear of the castle and a part of the vegetable garden.

Translations. In *Translations* he captures a Donegal community at the moment of transition from Gaelic to English, and removes the bandages from the ancient and festering wound that still weeps in Northern Ireland, in a lyrical and humane way. A writer worth reading.

In this part of the world towns have a central 'diamond', which the rest of us might call a square or triangle. Donegal also has its famous tweed. But what Donegal has most is unspoilt landscape with more sheep than people. Like the Donegal exiles, you may wish to return again and again.

Donegal town

On the way to Donegal town you will pass Bundoran and Ballyshannon. Bundoran, like Tramore in county Waterford is a beach resort when the sun decides to shine. Ballyshannon is built on the banks of the river Erne, where the river becomes tidal. In that tidal estuary is the islet Inis Saimer, where the *Lebor Gabala* (the Book of Invasions) tells us Partholón and his followers first arrived in Ireland from Scythia after the flood! Of the previous immigrants led by Cesair, who was related to Noah, only Fintan had survived the deluge. He is credited with witnessing all the subsequent invasions in the form of a salmon, an eagle and a hawk and is later called upon as a witness to all these events when the scribes came to write the *Lebor Gabala* in the twelfth century.

In the centre of Donegal town there is a monument to four men who continued the tradition of compiling manuscripts. In their seventeenth-century Annals of the Four Masters they tried to collect all they could of the old monastic manuscripts, including poetry and a new recension of the *Lebor Gabala,* just after the collapse of Gaelic Ireland. Donegal town's two main monuments, the O'Donnell Castle and the Franciscan friary, are interlinked with the Annals. The friary was founded by the O'Donnells in 1474 but with the defeat of O'Donnell and O'Neill at Kinsale in 1601 and their subsequent flight to the continent, Donegal was left leaderless and defenceless. The Franciscans were evicted from their friary and the four masters took up residence in a small peasant cottage near Bundoran. From there they journeyed around Ireland collecting and transcribing older manuscripts which they then digested and recompiled during the winter months, to make the Annals of the Four Masters. Their Annals date from the earliest times to the beginning of the seventeenth century and are an important source of Irish history. The chief 'master', the Franciscan lay brother Michael O'Clery, is buried in the Irish College of his order in Louvain, Belgium (then part of Spanish Flanders), a safe repository of many Irish manuscripts during the turbulent 1600s in Ireland.

The Donegal or O'Donnell Castle was first built and rebuilt in the fifteenth and sixteenth centuries. In 1616 it was granted to Sir Basil Brooke who carried out extensive renovations to the tower and installed a well-carved fireplace with his coat of arms. He also built the manor house adjacent to the tower which has some well-proportioned windows and doors.

Alternative routes

Lough Derg

Near the village of Laghy, on the Ballyshannon to Donegal road, is a turn off for Pettigo and Lough Derg, famous for Patrick's Purgatory, a small island in the lake which is a place of penitential pilgrimage for Irish catholics. In the medieval period it was renowned in christendom. Sinners were reputed to experience the horrors of hell in its underground cave. This belief grew from the tradition that St Patrick, by fasting for forty days in the cave, had expelled the devil from this place. One seventeenth-century poet wrote of his visit:

> _Naked, with little to eat,_
> _O body that caused all harm,_
> _your pains – Hell bent as you are –_
> _mean little to me tonight._

(translated from the Irish by Thomas Kinsella.)

The physically demanding pilgrimage lasts three full days, with only one meagre meal of black tea and dry bread per day, plus a sleepless vigil in the basilica on the first night. Pilgrims are asked to go barefoot during all their time on the island and are expected to walk on sharp stones. Special prayers are said at each 'penitential bed' or remains of the stone cell of the early Christian monks. The small island can be completely crowded with tours of pilgrims, and so is closed to non-pilgrims from the beginning of June to the middle of August, otherwise known as 'the pilgrimage season'. The average pilgrim appears to be getting older, with fewer younger people now taking part.

Very close to Pettigo, just across the border with Northern Ireland, is another island with two powerful and primitive sculptures. Boa

One of the pagan Celtic sculptures with two heads on Boa Island in Lower Lough Erne

Island, in Lower Lough Erne, is joined to the mainland by a bridge at each end. On its west side, in the ancient Christian graveyard of Caldragh, stand two stones with four faces. These pagan Celtic sculptures show probable deities with two heads and bodies joined together like Siamese twins, in the classical 'Janus' form. Surrounded by ferns and wild buttercup, these dualities of open mouths, almond eyes and crossed hands are intriguing. They embody the Celtic archetype of fundamental duality which the Celts saw as essential to all things. A day consisted of two parts, light and dark; a year of cold and warmth; and a life of birth and death. The Celtic warrior who told an ancient classical scholar that 'death was the centre of a long life' embodied this outlook and would be at ease with these sculptures.

Glencolumbkille

On the way to Glencolumbkille you pass through Killybegs, the most important fishing port in Ireland. Strangely, the Irish are not fish-eaters, despite living on an island, maybe because fish was always associated with penance and abstaining from meat on Fridays and certain 'fast' days. Whatever the reason, the national fishing fleet was not developed until the 1960s. Later, the advent of European Community membership has meant that countries with more developed fleets now have access to Irish waters to the detriment of the local industry.

The landscape becomes more rugged as you move west until you arrive at the water's edge and Glencolumbkille. White houses freckle the seaward slopes and beside the car park you will find a holiday home scheme and a folk museum. These two developments are the results of communal effort under the guidance of the local parish priest in the 1960s and 1970s. Faced with the loss of local youth through emigration, Fr James McDyer acted as catalyst and director of local action. In an interview with *The Irish Times* he said: 'You cannot wait until the people are ready for socialism. It may have to be forced on them as it was forced upon us in Glencolumbkille.' Socialism has never rested easily with most rural peoples, and Glencolumbkille is no exception. It is doubtful whether these 'socialist' or communal developments would have come to pass without the energy, vision and drive of Fr McDyer, coupled with his key role as local priest. Communal water schemes were installed by work-camps of Irish and other nationalities, along with local effort in the early 1960s, and from these successes spring the arts and crafts, holiday homes and folk museum you see today.

Hedged against a rocky hill, the museum consists of several replica cottages dating from different periods, equipped with appropriate furniture. The seemingly casual layout of the houses is based on the old *clachán* or cluster form of layout, remnants of which can still be seen on the Aran Islands and on Tory Island. Guided tours of the houses are available. Notice the different methods of securing the thatch at the roof edges from the Atlantic wind. The same wind, and lack of traditional edge detailing, revealed to me that the holiday homes have a tar roof under a fake thatch.

On 9 June, the feast-day of St Columbkille, the early Christian cross-slabs are visited by local people. The slabs are decorated with cross and geometric patterns and are spread out in the valley for over five kilometres. The easiest ones to visit are those adjacent to the Church of Ireland church. Megalithic tombs are also found locally but would not compare favourably with those in Sligo.

The road from Glencolumbkille to Ardara climbs, then dips, crossing hills and rivers, until you climb once again, before finally nose-diving the splendid Glengesh Pass on route to Ardara and Glenties. The Glenties catholic church is well sited and designed, with interesting gargoyles. Its architect, Liam McCormick, has crafted many fine churches in Donegal and this church from the 1970s is a quality design. The church was full for a wedding the day I was there and afterwards the grounds made a good backdrop for all the photographs. Using a loud-hailer the photographer called out instructions for the required family, bride-and-groom and guest group photographs.

Irish weddings are almost always church weddings with large numbers of invited relations and friends. Civil weddings are growing

The skill of roof-thatching stands out beautifully in this small turf-shed on the road to Ardara but even young lapsed catholics will have a church wedding either 'to please the parents' or because it has 'more style'. Either way, the celebrations that follow a wedding ceremony are pursued with devotion beyond duty. Grannies, aunts and uncles may be asked to sing their 'party piece' before the band or disco takes over. The formal end comes when the bride and groom are put in the centre of a dancing circle. They may be 'bounced', before finally leaving under an arch of arms and possibly to streams of tears loosened from parents in a spurt of emotion. A late-night party may develop for those with 'sticking power', and if good musicians are about. When it comes to enjoying themselves the Irish know how to do it better than most.

At Glenties you can keep to the coast or head inland via Fintown and postcard scenery to Letterkenny. Like Connemara, Donegal has so much physical beauty that no matter which way you go, there is untamed landscape at every turn.

The journey to Tory Island

Dungloe, or Dunglow as it is sometimes called on maps, is in the centre of an area known as 'the Rosses'. The Irish name *na Rosa,* meaning 'the headlands', is a good clue to part of its landscape. Streams vein the rock-strewn land and drain the random lakes and pools. Past Gweedore, where Irish is still spoken, you could turn towards cone-shaped Errigal mountain and drive through the magnificent scenery along Lough Nacung via Dunlewey, to Glenveagh National Park or continue to Gortahork (Magheraroarty Pier) and Tory Island.

Tory Island is neither easy to get to, live on nor get off. It is windswept and laid siege to frequently by the sea. Despite the hardship this island has been occupied for several thousand years. Mythology says that a powerful leader of the ancient Fomoire people, called Balor, lived on Tory. He is reputed to have had one eye on his forehead and another, which would cause death to those he looked upon, in the back of his head. This 'evil eye' required four men to raise its lid and was the Fomoirians secret weapon in battle, until Lug stopped its stare with a bullseye sling shot. The eastern Doon summit still bears the name Dún Balor, 'the fort of Balor', just in case you had any doubts about the story.

Beyond the Doon peninsula are eye-catching headlands with detached pinnacles of durable quartzite eroded into unusual shapes. The island has two villages simply called West Town and East Town. West Town has the shops, church, post office, health clinic and primary school, but East Town still has the most authentic *clachán* type settlement remaining in Ireland. Like the Blasket Island before it, Tory is producing a remarkable number of creative people who are literally drawing upon their surroundings for inspiration. These people are not writers but artists, whose naive style of painting radiates power and freshness. Oil and house paints are intermixed and applied by various techniques devised by the artists themselves. If you visit the Glebe Gallery near Churchill you may see some of these artists' works.

The ancient monolithic cross outside Cooley graveyard near Moville, Inishowen peninsula. The hole through the upper part of the shaft might have indicated the grave of a saint.

The remnants of St Columbkille's early Christian monastery are found close to the shore in West Town. A decapitated round tower still withstands Atlantic winds, while a seemingly decapitated cross stands on a plinth by the slipway. This T-shaped cross is called a tau cross and is one of only two existing in Ireland. You may have seen a sketch of the other tau cross from Killinaboy, county Clare, in the Burren Display Centre.

There is no strong sense of clock time as we know it on Tory and there is no rush to close the pub at the officially appointed time. I saw the wedding party of a local man and the community nurse led down the unpaved street by a drummer and an accordion player, the islanders stiff in their white starched shirts, the visitors intrigued by the display. I hope that this occasion gave hope to those who wish to stay and struggle against the beleaguering sea.

Glenveagh National Park and Glebe Art Gallery

Donegal has beautiful scenery but few focal points for enquiring visitors. Glenveagh National Park and the Glebe Art Gallery, however, are such focal points in northern Donegal. Both centres came about through donations by private individuals to the Irish people, the park from an Irish American millionaire, the art collection from an English artist and collector.

Glenveagh Castle was built in 1870 by John Adair, a notorious landlord, with the money of his American wife, to the design of a family relative called Trench. The design is more an exercise in superficial Gothic than a piece of developed architecture, yet its setting and gardens are exceptional. The gardens are the result of the imagination and dedication of its donating owner, Mr Henry

From the *Grianán* of Aileach, an impressive stone fort, you will have a fine view of the surrounding area of Derry and Donegal

McIlhenny, and his gardener. To reach the castle and gardens you must first abandon your car at the circular 'interpretative centre'. From there you are taken by minibus through part of the park to the castle and wonderful gardens. The reason for this is to confine cars to controlled areas and relieve environmental pressures on the ten-thousand-hectare park. Part of the park is covered with bog, heather and native woodlands, which support the largest herd of red deer in Ireland and so require additional conservation measures.

The Italian garden has laurels, pines, busts, sphinxes and, of course, Bacchus and Ceres, all immaculately maintained. The heather and rose gardens, the rhododendrons, and the fine lawn with specimen flowering trees are special, but the section that stole my heart was the *jardin potager*. Here ordinary vegetables are planted in row formation to their best possible effect and it is a tribute to those concerned with maintenance that this labour-intensive garden is kept as precisely as it was designed. Glenveagh National Park is beautiful, so don't miss it.

Close to Glenveagh, near the village of Churchill Hill, is Glebe Gallery. Remodelled outbuildings and stables house the extensive Derek Hill collection which includes an excellent selection by Tory Island painters. The refurbishment is well handled and the enclosed courtyard could act as a good display area for suitable sculptures. Glebe House, a former rectory from 1828 and once the residence of Derek Hill, is also open to the public.

It has been to the Irish nation's benefit that two men were so seduced by the beauty of Donegal that they lived here when it was neither fashionable nor profitable to do so, and in their generosity have bequeathed to Ireland treasures of landscape and art.

One of the two pillars flanking the early Christian Donagh cross in Carndonagh, Inishowen peninsula

Grianán of Aileach

This impressive stone fort from around 1700 BC, sits on top of a commanding hill overlooking the surrounding area of Derry and Donegal. According to the Annals of the Four Masters, it was the seat of power for the northern O'Neill kings from the fifth to the twelfth century and was destroyed by their enemies in AD 675 and 1101. The innermost wall was extensively reconstructed at the end of the last century, but you can still see the faint remains of the original concentric defence walls outside the present wall. Kuno Meyer's translation of an anonymous ancient Irish poem could apply to this place:

> *The Fort over against the oak-wood*
> *Once it was Bruidge's, it was Cathal's,*
> *It was Aed's, it was Cuiline's*
> *And it was Maelduin's;*
> *The Fort remains after each in his turn —*
> *And the kings asleep in the ground.*

Alternative route

Inishowen peninsula

If you still seek more Donegal landscape then a tour of Inishowen should give you what you are looking for.

Buncrana is a seaside town with wet weather 'amusement arcades' and a good beach. Carndonagh has a weathered early Christian cross of pleasant proportions and with good carving. On either side of the cross stand two pillars. One shows a man with a bell, probably a monk calling the faithful to prayer. The other shows a man with a sword and David with his harp. The churchyard behind the cross contains another carved pillar.

Close to Malin Head near a place called Five Finger Strand is a simple old church, its whitewash walls running out like white fingers to enclose a piece of consecrated land, in a bare landscape. Malin Head is special for one thing – its beautiful pebble beach. Storms and wild seas toss ashore a wide variety of water worn pebbles from as far away as Scotland, in exquisite colours and shapes.

Driving alongside Lough Foyle at dusk you will see across that gap

Small church in the open countryside near Five Finger Strand, Inishowen peninsula

of water the twinkling lights of Magilligan detention camp in county
Derry. At the border post at Muff you may or may not be detained
for a minute by Northern Ireland security forces before proceeding to
Derry city.

Coastal tour county Donegal

Route descriptions correspond with
map.

Route to Donegal town, Letterkenny
Cliffony – (N15) – Bundoran – Bal-
lyshannon – Ballintra – Laghy – *alter-
native 1*: (R232) Pettigoe – Lough Derg:
Patrick's Purgatory – Donegal town:
castle & friary – (N56) Milltown – *al-
ternative 2*: (R263) Killybegs – Carrick
– Glencolumbkille: folk museum –
Ardara – (N56) Glenties – (R250)
Fintown – Newmills – Letterkenny –
(N13) Pluck – Newtown Cunningham
– direction Bridge End: *Grianán* of
Aileach stone fort – (A2) Derry, county
Derry.

alternative 3: Tory Island, Glenveagh
Glenties – (N56) Maas – Dunglow –
Gweedore. For Tory Island: (N56) to
Gortahork, Magheraroarty Pier – Fal-
carragh – Dunfanaghy – Creeslough:
Doe Castle – (R251) Church Hill:
Glebe Art Gallery. For Glenveagh: from
Gweedore (R251) – Dunlewy – Glen-
veagh National Park.

alternative 4: Inishowen Peninsula
Bridge End – (R238) – Burnfoot –
Buncrana – Ballylifin – Carndonagh:
Donagh Cross – Malin – (R242) Ma-
lin Head – Malin – (R238) Culdaff –
Moville: Cooley graveyard – Carrow-
keel – Muff – (B194) Derry, county
Derry (Northern Ireland).

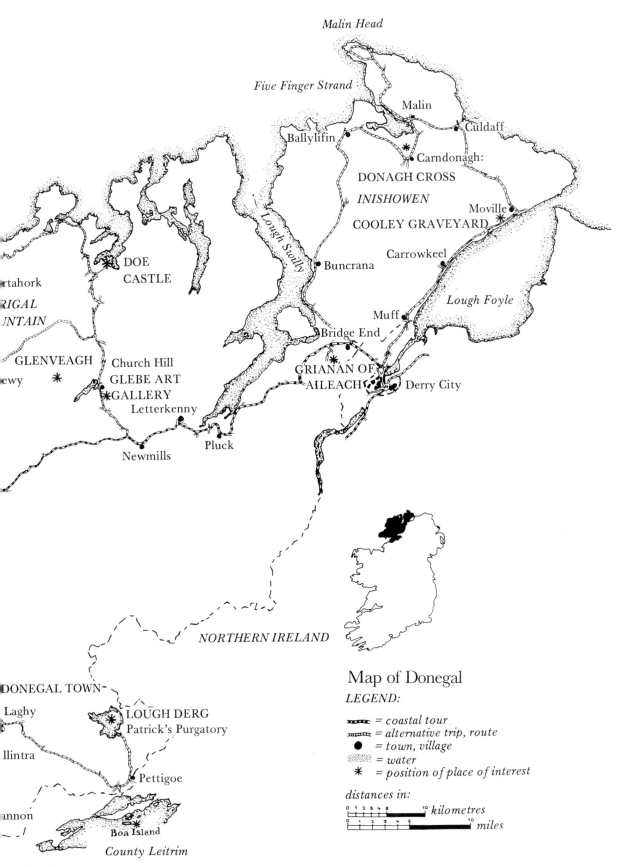

Malin Head

Five Finger Strand

Malin

Culdaff

Ballylifin

Carndonagh:

DONAGH CROSS

INISHOWEN

Moville

COOLEY GRAVEYARD

Lough Swilly

Carrowkeel

Buncrana

Lough Foyle

DOE
CASTLE

tahork

RIGAL
NTAIN

Muff

Bridge End

GLENVEAGH

Church Hill

GLEBE ART
GALLERY

ewy

GRIANAN OF
AILEACH

Derry City

Letterkenny

Pluck

Newmills

NORTHERN IRELAND

DONEGAL TOWN

Laghy

LOUGH DERG
Patrick's Purgatory

llintra

Pettigoe

annon

Boa Island

County Leitrim

ugh Melvin

Map of Donegal
LEGEND:

= coastal tour
= alternative trip, route
● = town, village
= water
✳ = position of place of interest

distances in:

0 1 2 3 4 5   10 kilometres
0 1 2 3 4 5   10 miles

Based on the Ordnance Survey by permission of the Government of the Republic of Ireland (Permit no. 4503).

Chapter 11
Northern Ireland

Northern Ireland contains beautiful scenery, especially in counties Antrim and Down. You should not be afraid to visit because of newspaper or television reports about bombs and killings. No visitor to Northern Ireland has yet been injured because most military activity takes place in ghetto areas, away from scenic locations. If you want to see such ghetto areas you should not try to photograph the security forces or use your camera in obvious unionist or nationalist areas without being accompanied by a known local person.

While I have travelled throughout Northern Ireland and have enjoyed the places and people I have seen, I do realise that many of you reading this book may prefer to wait for a more tranquil time to follow this part of the coast trip. In recognition of that fact and of the interest foreigners have in the 'Northern Ireland problem', I have given only an outline of the coastal route proposed along with a larger explanatory account of the present conflict.

Historical synopsis

Mention the name Ireland outside of Ireland and you get a bewildering collection of garbled half-truths or gross ignorance. Mention Northern Ireland and eyes either glaze over or eagerly want an 'explanation of the religious war'. It is difficult to give an explanation of what is essentially a political struggle, reinforced by a religious divide, but I will try to give a historical synopsis and the views held by the unionist/protestant and nationalist/catholic groups, along with the views of the British and Irish governments.

Successful plantation

After the defeat of the Irish chieftains at Kinsale in 1601,* and their subsequent flight to the continent, their lands were seized by the English crown. Settlers loyal to the crown, or 'planters' as the native Irish called them, were brought over from lowland Scotland and England and were given sections of confiscated land. Unlike previous attempts at mass colonisation in other parts of Ireland, this plantation was well organised and did succeed in its aims. These new settlers were protestant whereas the dispossessed Irish were catholics.

In 1641 the native Irish rebelled and sought revenge on their colonisers. Oliver Cromwell quashed the rebellion with a vengeance and confiscated even more land from the native Irish. When the catholic James II became king of England in 1685, there was great resentment among protestant English lords, who then invited the protestant Prince William of Orange from Holland to become king of England. James II fled to Ireland where he found support among the native Irish by promising them religious freedom and the return of

In the beginning of 'the Troubles' in Northern Ireland a part of Derry-city, called the bogside, was a 'no-go area' for security forces. This painted gable at the end of a former terrace of houses dates from the early 1970s and is deligently maintained as a nationalist symbol. Nearby thirteen civilians were shot by British paratroopers in January 1972.

There was great slaughter then, men, woman, child,
with fire and pillage of our timbered houses;
we had to build in stone for ever after.
That terror dogs us.
from 'The Colony' by John Hewitt (referring to the catholic uprising of 1641)

* See page 58

The soldier is proof against an argument but he is not proof against a bullet.
Thomas Francis Meagher, Dublin, 28 July 1846

confiscated lands. William of Orange followed James II to Ireland and defeated him and his Irish allies at the famous Battle of the Boyne on 12 July 1690. This day is still celebrated every year by unionists with 'Orange marches'.

United Irishmen rising

The next hundred years of Irish history saw 'penal laws' enacted against catholics (and later against presbyterians) in an effort to suppress any further uprisings. Anti-English political activists in Ireland, however, were mostly protestant. They were greatly influenced by the French Revolution of 1789 and the call for 'Liberty, Equality and Fraternity'. A group with similar aspirations called the 'United Irishmen' was formed in 1791. Their leader Wolfe Tone wrote that catholics and protestants should unite because 'the depression and slavery of Ireland were produced and perpetuated by the divisions existing between them'. With England at war with France, these French-inspired ideas were suspect and the United Irishmen were outlawed. Wolfe Tone sought French military aid but the revolution planned with French help was defeated in 1798. Tone's grave in Bodenstown, county Kildare, is at present the scene of small annual commemorations by the Irish government and *Sinn Féin* (the political wing of the IRA) in separate ceremonies, because he is seen as 'the father of Irish republicanism'.

'Home Rule is Rome Rule'

Ulster at the proper moment will resort to its supreme arbitrament of force. Ulster will fight, and Ulster will be right.
Lord Randolph Churchill, Larne, 22 February 1886

In the early 1800s Daniel O'Connell** achieved catholic emancipation (reform of political restrictions against catholics) in Ireland and Britain, but the Famine of 1845-50 wrecked Ireland. Later, in 1867, the nationalist Fenian uprising failed and was followed by a period of constitutional efforts in the British parliament to achieve 'Home Rule' for all Ireland. Gladstone, the Liberal British prime minister, introduced two Home Rule bills in 1886 and 1893, which were defeated. The unionists in Ireland opposed these bills and joined in an alliance with the British Conservative party. The 'Orange Order', first formed in 1795 and named after William of Orange, was revived and reorganised to oppose Home Rule which unionists declared would mean 'Rome Rule'. After the general election of 1910 the British Liberal party needed the support of the Irish parliamentary party to form a government. The Irish party gave the Liberals their support on condition that a Home Rule bill would be introduced. To overcome the known opposition of the British House of Lords, the parliament act of 1911 was enacted, which meant that a bill, once passed in the House of Commons, should within two years automatically become law. With the perceived threat of dreaded Home Rule, the unionists, under Carson and Craig, set about organising political and military resistance. Carson, who had been solicitor-general of England, spoke of defying the British parliament: 'We must be prepared the morning Home Rule passes, ourselves to become responsible for the government of

You are going to pass Home Rule… by a pure act of force…Your act of force will be resisted by force.
Sir Edward Carson, House of Commons, 8 August 1911

** *See page 71/72*

the Protestant province of Ulster.' In September 1912 some two hundred thousand unionists signed the 'Solemn League and Covenant', whereby they pledged allegiance to the king of England, but stated they would use 'all means which may be found necessary to defeat the present conspiracy to set up a Home Rule parliament in Ireland, and in the event of such a parliament being forced upon us to refuse to recognise its authority.'

In January 1913 the Home Rule bill was passed by the house of Commons but rejected by the Lords, so that under the parliament act it could not pass automatically till 1914. The Home Rule bill did not allow for Irish independence, but rather provided a parliament in Dublin to deal with purely Irish affairs; however, matters of defence, foreign policy, customs, etc. would still be administered from London.

The Orange Lodges (units of the Orange Order) formed a unified army called the Ulster Volunteer Force (UVF) and brought in arms from Germany. In response, nationalists formed their own volunteer force to defend Home Rule. A civil war seemed possible as 1914 dawned. In March 1914 British officers in Ireland declared that they would accept dismissal from the army rather than obey an order to enforce Home Rule. In the summer of 1914 the Home Rule bill received the king's signature, but the First World War broke out in August 1914 and the bill was deferred for the duration of the war.

On 12 July the unionists celebrate the Battle of the Boyne every year with their Orange marches. This is a sash that is worn on such a march.

A Belfast street rhyme around 1912
Sir Edward Carson had a cat
That sat upon a stool,
And every time it caught a rat
It shouted: No Home Rule.

Easter rising

Large numbers of Irish volunteers fought for Britain in the war in the hope of winning a favourable response from Britain when it was over. A small minority of National Volunteers refused to fight for 'King nor Kaiser'. They planned a revolution for Easter 1916 in the cause of a completely independent Irish republic. Less than a thousand National Volunteers took part, and fighting was confined to Dublin city were it lasted for a week. Fifteen leaders of the rising were shot for treason by a British army firing squad, after they surrendered. Pearse, one of the executed leaders, had declared: 'Life springs from death; and from the graves of patriot men and women spring living nations...' His prophecy came to pass, because the executions won sympathy for the Volunteers' cause and what had been an unpopular revolution suddenly became a focus for future action.

Sinn Féin, meaning Ourselves (alone), became a political force and completely replaced the old Irish parlimentary party in the general election of 1918, which coincided with the end of the war. It was now clear that Home Rule would not be enough to pacify nationalist aims. The Northern unionists pressed a new claim for a separate parliament for Belfast, while elected nationalists refused to take their Westminster (London) seats. In early 1919 nationalists made a 'Declaration of Independence' and tried to set up their own courts, banks, etc. This was resisted by the British authorities. Sporadic nationalist guerilla fighting began. In 1920, six counties of Ireland were given a separate parliament while guerilla activity increased in the remainder of Ireland. In 1921, after a bloody struggle involving

I am against this treaty, not because I am a man of war, but a man of peace. I am against this treaty because it will not end the centuries of conflict between the two nations of Great Britain and Ireland.
Éamon de Valera, 19 December 1921

some sixty thousand British troops and para-military forces, a treaty was offered.

The nation splits

Under the terms of the treaty Northern Ireland was to remain separate from the remainder of Ireland, while the rest of the country would become a 'Free State' within the British Empire and would also give an oath of allegiance to the king of England. Irish nationalists split on the treaty issue: hard-line republicans, led by de Valera, wanted complete independence from Britain and did not accept the setting up of a separate state in Northern Ireland, while the 'Free Staters', under the leadership of Michael Collins, were in favour of accepting the terms of the treaty. A year long civil war ensued with victory for those who accepted the treaty. Meanwhile, Northern Ireland nationalists, who comprised one-third of the electorate, decided to declare for an Irish state and flew the Irish flag in city and country areas under their control. They claimed that they were ceding from Northern Ireland in the same way that unionists had ceded from the remainder of Ireland. The unionist government changed the method of election, altered election boundaries and set up a paramilitary police group called B-Specials to counteract the nationalists. Riots and sectarian killings followed, before an uneasy peace was enforced. While Northern and Southern Ireland developed along different socio-economic paths until the 1960s, secretarian and political trouble erupted sporadically in Northern Ireland in both the 1930s and 1950s. The B-Specials were used to enforce unionist law and order, while the revised boundaries and system of election kept even nationalist cities like Derry (officially Londonderry) under unionist city council control.

Republic of Ireland declared

The historic task of this generation is to secure the economic foundation of independence.
Sean Lemass, parliament speech, 3 June 1959

During the 1930s to late 1950s period, the Southern Irish government was predominently under de Valera and his *Fianna Fáil* party, which he had set up following a split with *Sinn Féin*. De Valera, who had been on the losing side of the Civil War, pursued a policy of self-determination and the breaking of formal links with Britain. Southern Ireland remained neutral during the Second World War and in 1949 declared itself a republic. The insular and socially conservative outlook of Southern Ireland continued into the late 1950s, when the prime minister Seán Lemass initiated an economic drive which changed living standards for the better. The Southern Irish economy began to catch up with the British-supported living standards of Northern Ireland and social attitudes started to liberalise. A similar process of liberalisation seemed to occur in Northern Ireland under its new prime minister, Captain Terence O'Neill. In 1965 an historic meeting took place when the two Irish prime ministers met in Belfast and discussed areas of mutual interest and economic development. For the first time since the partition of Ireland there was dialogue between the two governments.

Civil rights movement

In 1964 the Rev Ian Paisley, a sectarian protestant demagogue, was the cause of riots in Belfast. That same year saw the establishment of the Northern Ireland Civil Rights Association (NICRA) which had been inspired by the black civil rights organisation in America. The aims of the NICRA were electoral reform, proper housing for all and the end of sectarian discrimination in Northern Ireland. Paisley increased his agitation against the NICRA, which he saw as undermining the unionist position. In 1966 a catholic barman was murdered by a protestant paramilitary group called the Ulster Volunteer Force or UVF (called after the 1912 unionist army), which was outlawed as a result.

The civil rights groups continued to press their just demands, but the hard-line unionists in O'Neill's government would not allow any concessions. A large civil rights march was announced for October 1968 in Derry city, but it was banned by the unionist government. Television cameras captured a brutal police baton charge and instantly Northern Ireland became an international news topic.

In April 1969 O'Neill resigned, and with him went the liberal face of unionism. In his resignation speech he said 'I have tried to break the chains of ancient hatreds. I have been unable to realise during my period in office all that I had sought to achieve. Whether now it can be achieved in my lifetime I do not know. But one day these things will be and must be achieved.'

Escalation and alienation in the North

Following unionist parades, riots broke out in Derry in August 1969. Security forces were unable to control the situation and in some instances resorted to indiscriminate gunfire.

In Belfast nationalists were burnt out of their homes in unionist-dominated areas. Nationalist areas retaliated and political-cum-religious ghettos were created as a result. The situation got so out of control that the British army was sent in to restore order. At first the army was welcomed by nationalists as a peace-keeping force, but gradually it was seen as an instrument of the still functioning unionist government. The paramilitary Irish Republican Army (IRA), which had been dormant up until this period, now put itself forward as the defender of the nationalist ghettos against the UVF and the British army. Internment without trial was introduced in 1971 by the Belfast government and this caused further alienation of the nationalist community. In January 1972 British army paratroopers shot thirteen unarmed anti-internment marchers near 'Free Derry Corner' in an incident which has become known as Bloody Sunday.

A tremendous wave of nationalist feeling swept over Ireland. The British Embassy in Dublin was burnt to the ground after a huge demonstration against the Bloody Sunday killings. The unionist government was replaced by a British minister who made some reforms but the situation seemed to have gathered a momentum of its own. The IRA started a bombing campaign which has continued despite all security efforts. The unionist paramilitaries responded by

To every cocked ear, expert in its greed,
His battered signature subscribes 'No Pope'.
The goatskins sometimes plastered with his blood.
The air is pounding like a stethoscope.
from 'Orange Drums, Tyrone, 1966' by Seamus Heaney

Unity has got to be thought of as a spiritual development which will be brought about by peaceful means.
'Sean Lemass looks back' *The Irish Press,* 28 January 1969

You cannot talk peace until the enemy surrenders, and the enemy is the Roman Catholic Church.
Rev Ian Paisley, *The Irish Times,* 23 August 1969

The Catholics have been interfering in Ulster affairs since 1641.
Rev Ian Paisley, *The Irish Times,* 30 August 1969

And did we come into our own
When, minus muse and lexicon,
We traced in August sixty-nine
Our imaginary Peace Line
Around the burnt-out houses of
The Catholics we'd scarcely loved,
Two Sisyphuses come to budge
The sticks and stones of an old grudge
'Letter to Derek Mahon' by Michael Longley

He was blown to bits
Out drinking in a curfew
Others obeyed, three nights
After they shot dead
The thirteen men in Derry.
PARAS THIRTEEN, the walls said,
BOGSIDE NIL. That Wednesday
Everyone held
His breath and trembled.
from 'Casualty' by Seamus Heaney

assassinating catholics.

A ray of hope appeared in 1974 when a power-sharing coalition between nationalists and a section of the unionists was set up. Immediately militant unionists opposed this government and organised political strikes to cause its downfall. Direct rule from London was reintroduced after only a few months of coalition government. The coalition parties blamed lack of official British support against the political and paramilitary strikers for the collapse of the power-sharing experiment.

IRA hunger strikes

At the beginning of the 1980s the hunger strikes of IRA prisoners demanding continuation of political status again focused media attention on Northern Ireland. Following the deaths of many hunger strikers nationalist opinion in the ghetto areas hardened, and support for the IRA and its political party, *Sinn Féin* (not to be confused with the earlier party of the same name) increased considerably at the expense of the constitutional nationalists, the Social Democratic and Labour Party (SDLP).

New Ireland Forum

With an increasingly polarising political situation the major political parties of the republic of Ireland and the SDLP from Northern Ireland met in the New Ireland Forum in 1984 and produced the Forum Report, which states that the aim of nationalists in all Ireland is for unity with consent, and which promises unionists an equitable role in some agreed form of united Ireland. The traditional answer of 'no surrender' is the only unionist reply. The IRA and *Sinn Féin* oppose the Forum Report as being too soft and they continue to seek through 'the armalite [rifle] and ballot box' to achieve their united Ireland. They claim to seek a 'socialist republic' although their aims and attitudes are more militarist/nationalist than socialist. They also seek the overthrow of the government of the Republic of Ireland, where the IRA is an illegal organisation.

The majority of Northern Irish nationalists support the SDLP, but the urban working-class ghettos have been won over by *Sinn Féin* (the political wing of the IRA) who claim that the only way nationalists have ever gained anything from a biased British government has been through the use of physical military force. *Sinn Féin* also claim to be the only true inheritors of Irish republicanism. The SDLP have been driven to become more 'green' or nationalist during the long crisis since 1970 by unionist intransigence and unsympathetic British government policies. They now demand a solution within the frame work of a united Ireland, whereas in the early 1970s they would have settled for an internal Northern Ireland arrangement which recognised the nationalist viewpoint. The SDLP leader, John Hume, a man of considerable intellect and political ability, states that Britain cannot blame 'tribal warfare' for the situation. He has asked Britain to remove the 'guarantee' of British

Mr Kane praised Martin Luther and John Wycliffe was mentioned in a second resolution. 'We are pledged to uphold the Protestant religion and to oppose any encroachment on our heritage, regardless of the cost.'
Report on Twelfth July March, *The Irish Times,* 13 July 1984

support to the unionist cause as long as the unionists are in a majority. Hume argues that the unionist majority is 'artficially created' and that the 'guarantee' only perpetuates unionist inflexibility and refusal to enter into 'meaningful dialogue' with their nationalist neighbours. Hume claims that until unionists are obliged by Britain, their big brother as it were, to enter such a dialogue the cycle of violence and instability will continue.

who would connive
in civilized outrage
yet understand the exact
and tribal, intimate revenge.
from 'Punishment' by Seamus Heaney

'Ulster is British'

The unionists say they will not be bullied into a united Ireland by anyone and will resist like their forefathers. The monolithic Unionist party, which had ruled Northern Ireland since its foundation, split when Britain introduced direct rule. The Official Unionist party (OUP) represents middle-class unionists, while Paisley's Democratic Unionist party (DUP) draws its main support from working-class unionist ghettos and ultra-conservative farmers and professionals. The small Alliance party represents moderate unionist opinion, those who whould support power sharing with nationalists, but not a united Ireland. The OUP and DUP insist that they have a 'democratic right' to rule Northern Ireland because they are in the majority and they are not prepared to share executive power 'with those whose aim is to have a United Ireland', because 'Ulster is British'.

There were angry scenes when Mr Kerr [*Sinn Féin* Councillor] took the chair and addressed the meeting in Irish. Unionists shouted: 'Speak English. Shut up you Fenian bastard. No Pope here. No bastards here, you want your throat cut Kerr, you Fenian bastard.'
'North's councils in the aftermath', *The Irish Times,* 13 June 1985

The unionists made great play in the past of the fact that Southern Ireland did not have the welfare state that Britain offered. Now that the gap is closing it is the older argument of 'Rome Rule' and the historical unionist 'right' that is more frequently used. The 'Rome Rule' argument is less convincing now than it used to be, because the very young population of Southern Ireland is becomming more pluralist in outlook. However, the Rev Ian Paisley has stated that even if he wrote the constitution of a united Ireland, he still would not want anything to do with it.

The once prosperous industrial cities of Belfast and Derry are now in serious decline with huge levels of unemployment. The British government now provides one-third of Northern Ireland's budget. Unemployment in nationalist areas is over twice that in unionist areas. Northern Island is also suffering a 'brain drain' as many university graduates leave the province in search of work and social harmony.

The Anglo-Irish Agreement

The Southern Irish government has sought dialogue and agreement with Britain since the collapse of the power sharing experiment in 1974.

The British government's attitude and interest in Northern Ireland since then has varied according to IRA/*Sinn Féin* activity. The electoral advance of *Sinn Féin* following the hunger strikes in the early 1980s caused grave concern to the British and Irish governments. Constitutional nationalists formulated the New Ireland Forum and pressed their case with the British government. Following a year of negotiations the Anglo-Irish Agreement was signed in 1985. This agreement formally gave the Southern Irish government a consultative role in Northern Ireland affairs in return for even more security co-operation. Different political groups have different interpretations of the agreement. The British government pushes the security aspects and restates its 'guarantee' to unionists that Norther Ireland will remain part of Britain as long as the majority in the province so wish. The Irish government emphasises its formal consultative role and hails the agreement as an historical precedent. Northern nationalists, who vote SDLP, support it because their leader John Hume has played a mayor part in its formulation and they seek to reverse *Sinn Féin* electoral gains. *Sinn Féin* leaders and supporters see it as 'window dressing' and a betrayal of traditional 'republican' aims. The unionists oppose the agreement because they claim it will lead to united Ireland. They accuse the British government of betrayal and pledge total opposition to any involvement of Southern Ireland in their 'internal affairs'.

Whether the agreement works will depend on astute and sensitive political decisions, their successful implementation and the containment of IRA and unionist opposition for a sufficient time to allow political and security progress to develop. Only time will tell.

Most young Southern Iris people want some solution to work, because they feel that the situation in the North could overflow and bring back less sophisticated, more primitive Civil War type politics to the Republic.

Consequences of conflict for North and South

Where tongues lie coiled, as under flames lie wicks,
Where half of us, as in a wooden horse
Were cabin'd and confined like wily Greeks,
Besieged within the siege, whispering morse.
from 'Whatever you Say Say Nothing'
by Seamus Heaney

If you judge a country or government by how it treats its minorities, be they political, social, disabled or handicapped groups, then Northern Ireland has performed very poorly under unionist control. As a majority in Northern Ireland, but a minority in the island of Ireland, unionists have exhibited a very conservative, triumphalist and unyielding political attitude to their nationalist neighbours. They claim that if the security forces 'were allowed to root out' or 'terrorise the terrorists', meaning the IRA, the province would be peaceful. This seems an unbelievable and naive statement.

What is clear is that Ireland, North and South, has suffered economically because of partition and the present conflict. Border areas on both sides are among the most disadvantaged in the EEC. The border counties represent twenty per cent of the total land area in the whole island and about fifteen per cent of its population. The Republic of Ireland could build over two hundred schools a year with the money it spends on border and paramilitary surveillance. Smuggling and racketeering in border areas also encourages a very large 'black' economy.

The self esteem and national potential of Ireland as a whole is being undermined by the conflict, and for that reason alone some workable solution must be found to stop the haemorrhage and the clotting of communal hate. The pages of history don't have to be torn out but they should be turned over.

An heroic style wall mural in nationalist
west Belfast

Coastal route

Derry city

St Columcille founded a monastery here in 546 when the area was an
oakwood. The Irish name _Doire_ means 'a place of oaks'. When the
saint went as a missionary to Scotland he often wrote of Derry and its
oak trees:

> _My Derry, my little oak-grove,_
> _My dwelling and my little cell,_
> _O living God that art in Heaven above,_
> _Woe to him who violates it!_

(translated from the Irish by Kuno Meyer)

Derry has been violated many times since this poem was written. It
gained the prefix London in the seventeenth century and became
Londonderry because twelve London companies undertook to bring
Scottish and English settlers there. The original name Derry was
restored by the nationalist city council in 1984.

The old port of Derry is compact and pleasant and lies on the west
side of the river Foyle. There is a certain visual similarity between
Cork and Derry because both are built on hills. The tourist office is
in Foyle Street.

Mussenden Temple and Mountsandel

Close to Downhill is Mussenden Temple built by Bishop Hervey in
1783. It is almost a replica of the Temple of Vespa in Tivoli. Built by
Italian craftsmen, it is named after Mrs Mussenden, a cousin and

close friend of the bishop. There are pathways full of rhododendrons and glens of oak and ash nearby if you get tired of looking out to sea from the cliff-top temple.

A kilometre south of Coleraine, at the end of a long stretch of forest is a huge mound called Mountsandel. Archaeological excavation has found much evidence from 7000 BC when it was a mesolithic site. Later the mound became the royal seat for King Fintan and later still a Norman Fort.

Dunluce Castle, Bushmills, Giant's Causeway

Dunluce Castle has perched on its coastal rock for seven hundred years. Two of the original four circular towers remain but the main ruins date from the seventeenth century.

Bushmills is famous for its whiskey of which Special Old Black Bush is my favourite. Along with other Irish whiskeys, Black Bush compares more than favourably with Scottish or American whisky. I don't know how the town stays sober.

In the last century the Giant's Causeway was thought to be one of the 'wonders of the world' and in some ways it is. Formed from basaltic rock which cooled and split into regular prismatic shapes, it stepped out of the sea to build an irregular honeycomb of columns some seventy million years ago. Yet this basalt is the youngest rock in Ireland although the writer Thackeray thought it was a leftover from the creation of the world – 'a remnant of chaos'. How he thought geometric regularity to be 'chaos' I don't know; maybe he had been to Bushmills before he came or perhaps he had only one eye open, like the mythological Fomorians after whom the rocks take their Irish name meaning the Fomorian's stepping stones.

Larne, Carrickfergus and Belfast

The coast of Antrim is full of cliffs, headlands and a succession of beautiful views. At Cushendall you could detour into one of the nine glens of Antrim where the mountains run back, parallel to each other, from the narrow sea channel to Scotland. The word Scots derives from the fourth-century Irish verb 'to raid'. The Latin name *Scotia* was first given to Ireland, from where the raiders came. It was not until the eleventh century that its meaning transferred to mean the country now called Scotland.

Larne was a safe port much used by the Vikings. In 1914 the unionists landed guns from Germany to oppose Home Rule. Further south is Carrickfergus, supposed to be called after Fergus MacEre, king of north-east Ireland and Scotland and one of the 'raiders', no doubt! Carrickfergus Castle is excellently preserved, with its ancient portcullis still existing after hundreds of years of colourful history, which will be completely explained on a conducted tour.

Belfast was called 'Devout, profane and hard' by its poet Louis MacNeice. City of bomb and bullet, soda farls and baps, it grew up as a settler's fort in the seventeenth century. In the nineteenth century its open spaces disappeared under linen mills and factories.

I was born in Belfast between the mountains and the gantries
To hooting of lost sirens and the clang of trams:
Thence to Smoky Carrick in County Antrim
Where the bottle-neck harbour collects the mud that jams
The little boats beneath the Norman Castle.
From 'Carrickfergus' by Louis MacNeice

Shipbuilding, sectarian riots, the Falls and the Shankill grew and were nurtured here in the industrial smog of Victorian progress. It is a place of close, some might say closed, communities. The city suffered bombs in the 1970s, but before that it suffered a mean industrial revolution, and since the 1970s it has been bisected by motorways. Except for a few buildings such as the Grand Opera House and the Crown Liquor Saloon, both on Great Victoria Street, the city is rather grey and utilitarian in design. But its people are tough, friendly and outspoken.

The city centre is pedestrianised for security reasons but otherwise tries to ignore the 'Troubles' that surround it. Taking a black taxi – they are run like miniature buses – to see the nationalist enclaves is a very depressing experience. Surrounded by army and police fortresses and watched over by helicopters, these areas endure rather than live. The Botanic Gardens and the university on the other side of town are a world apart.

Down there at the end of the melancholy lough
Against the lurid sky over the stained water
Where hammers clang murderously on the girders
Like crucifixes.
From 'Belfast' by Louis MacNeice

Ulster Folk Museum near Bangor

Some twelve kilometres from Belfast at Cultra, set in a sixty-hectare park, you will find a well-presented folk museum. Each building has its own caretaker/guide and a turf fire if there is a chimney. There are no 'Do not touch' signs, and visitors have responded to this liberalism in an adult manner. My only criticism of this well-run museum is the insipid tea and plastic food of the snack bar.

Mount Stewart Estate near Newtownards

Mount Stewart is a good example of an eighteenth-century house to which an exuberant group of gardens have been added or redesigned in the twentieth century. Former house of the marquesses of Londonderry it is now open to the public. The house is a bit austere but the interior spaces are imposing and together with the gardens have played host to a gallery of famous and infamous people. The gardens are a gardener's delight. The shamrock garden has an Irish harp fashioned out of a yew tree as an example of topiary and not so far away the red hand, symbol of Ulster (the northern province of Ireland, which includes the six Northern Ireland counties and three others), is set within the green lawn. There are other formal and informal gardens, ponds, lakes, terraces and woodlands to be explored. The Temple of the Winds is based on the Athens model of the same name.

Across the narrow strait from Portaferry and close to Strangford is an example of what can happen when husband and wife disagree about their house. The front or husband's side is classical while the back or wife's side is Strawberry Hill 'Gothic'. Inside the rooms are divided likewise in style. The house was built for lord and lady Bangor and is situated in the demesne of Castle Ward.

NORTH CHANNEL

GIANT'S CAUSEWAY

Ballingtoy

DUNLUCE CASTLE

Dimseverick

Downhill BUSHMILLS

Portrush Ballycastle

MUSSENDEN TEMPLE

GLENS OF ANTRIM

Glebe Coleraine

Lough Foyle MOUNTSANDEL

LIMAVADY

Cushendall

DERRY CITY

County Derry

Carnlough

County Antrim

Larne

Strabane Glynn

NORTHERN IRELAND

Ballycarr

Newtownstewart

C

Cultra

Omagh UL.
FOLK

Lough Neagh BELFAST

Aughnacloy

County Down

Clough

Monaghan

Newcastle

Border between Northern Ireland Newry
and Republic of Ireland

Map of Northern Ireland
(Derry, Antrim, Down)

MOURNE MOUNTAINS

Castleblayney

Based upon the Ordnance Survey map with the sanction of
the Controller of HM Stationery Office, Crown Copyright
reserved.

Cullaville

to Carlingford

to Dundalk Kilkeel

Newcastle

This town with its beach is the seaside resort of the north-east and is well located for a detour through the beautiful Mourne Mountains. Tolleymore Forest Park offers walks, arboretum, café and camping and is a pleasant setting but avoid Sunday when it is crowded with visitors. If you take the coast road there are many pleasant views and as you turn west along Carlingford Lough, the Cooley peninsula lies across the inlet of the sea.

Coastal tour Northern Ireland
Route descriptions correspond with map

The tour along the coast of the counties Derry, Antrim and Down is marked in the code of 'alternative route'.
Derry city (A2) – Ballykelly – (B69) Glebe – (A2) Downhill: Mussenden Temple – Coleraine – (A54, direction Kilrea): Mountsandel – (A54) Coleraine – (A29) Portrush: Dunluce Castle – (B145) Bushmills – (A2, B140) Giant's Causeway – Dimseverick – (A2) Ballingtoy – (B15) Ballycastle – (A2) Cushendall – Carnlough – Larne – Glynn – (B90) Ballycarry – (A2) Carrickfergus: castle – Belfast – (A2) Hollywood – Cultra: Ulster Folk Museum – Bangor (A21) – Newtownards: Mount Stewart House & Gardens (A20) – Kircubbin – Portaferry – Strangford – (A2) Ardglass – Clough – Newcastle – Kilkeel – Newry – (B79, R173) Carlingford, Cooley peninsula, county Louth.

Inland tour via Monaghan to Dundalk, county Louth
Derry city (A5) – Strabane – Newtownstewart – Omagh – Aughnacloy – (N2) Monaghan – Castleblaney – (N53) Cullaville – (A37, N53) Dundalk, county Louth.

LEGEND:
= coastal tour
= alternative trip, route
= town, village
= water
= position of place
of interest

ances in:
kilometres
miles

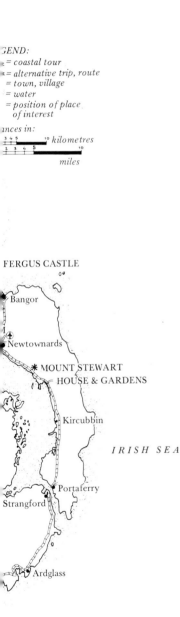

FERGUS CASTLE

Bangor

Newtownards

MOUNT STEWART
HOUSE & GARDENS

Kircubbin

IRISH SEA

Portaferry

Strangford

Ardglass

Chapter 12

Counties Louth and Meath

Some of the best farming land in Ireland can be found in these counties. The same land attracted successive settlers to Ireland, so that it is not surprising to find neolithic, Celtic, Christian and Norman buildings, legends and art work juxtaposed.

Those wealthy and well organised neolithic farmers built their burial chambers before the Egyptians, on the banks of the river Boyne, and like the Egyptian pyramids their burial mounds are a cause of wonder. When the Celts arrived they recognised these unique mounds as something special and assimilated them into their culture. Some became royal enclosures such as the Hill of Tara, while others became the dwelling places of Celtic gods. Tara was the great assembly place of the Celts and the following extract from a long poem in the ancient Book of Rights gives us an insight into what went on. This extract is taken from the book *Celtic Mysteries, the ancient religion* by John Sharkey:

> *When the harvest month began*
> *After a lapse of three years span,*
> *Daily seeking victor's praise*
> *Riders racing through seven days.*
> *Settlements of tax and due,*
> *Legal cases to review,*
> *Laws to publish and declare,*
> *This the business of the fair.*

The druids and poets had a privileged position in the very aristocratic Celtic society and poetic study became a hereditary occupation which lasted into the late medieval period. The axe-wielding O'Daly from Lissadell in Sligo was a descendant of such a family.

The magnificent Newgrange burial mound was designated as the dwelling place of the Celtic god of love, Oenghus, whose father was Daghdha, the chief god. Daghdha was also father of the goddess Brigid who was responsible for sacred wells, livestock, the home, poetry and traditional learning. When the Christian missionaries arrived they christianised Brigid and made her a saint, expert in the same functions as her pagan counterpart. Her feast day was put on the first of February, the pagan Celtic festival of *Imbolg* (lactation of ewes) and so a pagan goddess and festival were assimilated with comparative ease. The Christian *Lives of the Saints* states that the new St Brigid (patroness of Ireland) hung her wet cloak on the sun's rays and that her house at Faughart, county Louth appeared ablaze to onlookers. A monastery attributed to her in Kildare was once the place of a pagan sacred fire. Medieval history tells us that a perpetual flame was kept burning here by her Christian followers until the arrival of the Normans, thus continuing, but altering, an older pagan ritual.

Now until the coming of Patrick speech was not suffered to be given in Ireland but to three: to a historian for narration and the relation of tales; to a poet for eulogy and satire; to a Brehon lawyer for giving judgment according to the old tradition and precedent. But with the coming of Patrick every speech of these men is under the yoke of the men of the white [blessed] language, that is, the scriptures.
from *Senchus Mór* or 'The Great Tradition'

Opposite page: The Newgrange tumulus, including its entrance, two of the beautifully carved kerb stones, the plan and some of the intriguing decorations in and outside this passage grave. These decorations are a source of mystery and have not yet been explained by scholars satisfactorily.

The Celts divided Ireland into five provinces, four of which exist today in Leinster, Munster, Connacht and Ulster. The kingdom of Meath was the fifth kingdom. The old Irish word for province *coiced,* meant a fifth or a centre with four corners.

Until the seventeenth century poets wrote poems comparing heroic Celtic heroes with Christian saints, often to the disadvantage of the latter.
Patrick: Oisin, you sleep too long
Rise up and hear the psalm
now your strength and health are gone
and your fierce fighting over.
Oisin: My strength and health are gone
because Fionn's troops are dead.
No music but theirs I love.
I have no care of priests.
(anonymous poet, translated from the Irish by Thomas Kinsella)

This fire cult of the pagan Celts was broken by the other patron saint of Ireland, Patrick, when he lighted a fire on the Hill of Slane when it was forbidden to do so by the druids. The hills of Tara, Tailte and Slane were sites for ritual pagan fires in the ancient kingdom of Meath. By breaking the druid's regulations, Patrick brought himself to the notice of the high king at Tara, whom he duly converted to Christianity. Today, the Hill of Tara contains the pagan *Lia Fáil,* a phallic fertility symbol that supposedly shrieked when the new king was accepted. A crumbling statue of St Patrick stands nearby. This one site contains neolithic, pagan and Christian remains, the latter two in amusing juxtaposition.

When the Christian missionaries won over the people to Christianity by tolerant attitudes to their pagan gods and rituals they then ousted the pagan priests or druids. The poets were also in danger of losing their special position at the *Druim Ceat* Synod in AD 575 but Columcille, himself a poet with royal relations, intervened and secured the poets' future for another thousand years.

The town of Trim, not far from where the Book of Kells was illuminated, marks the extension of the 'Pale', or area of complete Norman influence, until the Tudor conquests of the sixteenth and seventeenth centuries.

Cooley peninsula

Cooley is the lost peninsula of Ireland. Bypassed by the main Dublin/Belfast road and without its former holiday visitors from Northern Ireland, the peninsula has not developed as much as it could. The name Cooley is enshrined in the ancient *Táin Bo Cuailgne* or 'Cattle Raid of Cooley'. Queen Medb, whom we met in Sligo, sought to take by force the prize bull of Cooley, so that her riches and possessions would match her husband's.

The *Táin* saga is the oldest vernacular epic in western literature and was eventually written down by monks in various manuscripts from early Christian times to the medieval period. It is the Celtic equivalent of the Greek Iliad and, like that epic, was partly based on actual rivalry between Ulster (the northern province) and Connacht (the western province). The progress of armies and places of battle can still be found in placenames today. In fact, a discontinuous line of earthworks running from Bundoran in county Donegal to near Carlingford Lough, a distance of some 220 kilometres bears witness to the ancient rivalry. These earthworks (later called the 'Black Pigs' Dyke') date from the second century and were designed, not as a 'Hadrian Wall' * system of defence, but as protection against cattle-raiding. Cattle were the measure of wealth under the ancient Celtic system.

At first reading, the *Táin,* like the Iliad, appears to be a fantastic story of impossible deeds. Behind the overshadowing dramatic exploits is information about social institutions, dress, fosterage, festivals, warfare, religion, etc, which have proved invaluable to Celtic scholars. The Celtic poets were an important social institution and in the *Táin* saga they are called upon to forsee the future. Indeed the original meaning of the Irish word *file* was 'seer' before it came to

Celtic representation of a sacred bull, incised on a stone slab, from Burghead, Morayshire, Scotland

* *Former wall between England and Scotland.*

Cottage on the road to Balbriggan

mean poet in later times. The ability 'to see' the invisible and obtain
prior knowledge was the domain of the Celtic *file*. Queen Medb calls
on Fedelm, woman poet of Connacht to use her *imbas forasna,* the
light of foresight:

I see a battle: a blond man
with much blood about his belt
and a hero-halo round his head
His brow is full of victories…

He towers on the battlefield
in breastplate and red cloak.
Across the sinister chariot-wheel
the Warped Man deals death
– that fair form I first beheld
melted to a mis-shape.

(translation by Thomas Kinsella)

Cúchulainn, the hero and defender of Ulster is the 'blond man' with
severed heads hanging from his belt. The 'hero-halo' indicates his
divine aspects when he is seized by his 'warp spasm'. He changes
from a beardless youth whom no one would take seriously to a
warrior 'making dense massacre'. Cúchulainn's shape-shifting is
another Celtic archetype and parallels that of the Brown Bull of
Cooley and the White Bull of Connacht, who were conceived by rival
deities who transformed themselves into various fish and animal
shapes before causing the conception of the two bulls. Their rivalry is
concluded when the two bulls fight and mortally wound each other.

In transcribing the oral stories the Christian scribes did censor those aspects they considered too pagan, but, realising the wide audience these stories had, they attached Christian blessings to their versions of the stories. The Book of Leinster version of the *Táin* ends with 'A blessing on everyone who will memorise the *Táin* faithfully in this form, and not put any other form on it.'

In other stories pagan Celtic heroes and saints meet and discuss the new religion in order to bond together the pagan and Christian traditions. Again the Irish language gives us a further clue. The favourite word for an historian in Irish at that time was *fer comgne* meaning 'synchroniser'. The bonding and synchronising worked and the great Christian art works and schools of learning such as Clonmacnois are its testimony.

The walk across the Cooley mountains follows part of the *Táin* route and links Ravensdale Forest with Carlingford town via Slieve Foye forest. Beautiful views of Carlingford Lough and the Mourne mountains can be had from Slieve Foye and Claremount cairn.

Forests now account for six per cent of Ireland's land surface compared to just one half of a per cent at the beginning of the twentieth century. Until the seventeenth century Ireland was heavily forested, but it was denuded for shipbuilding and mining. The early 1950s saw Seán MacBride (the only man to receive both Nobel and Lenin Peace prizes) institute a dramatic increase in forest planting, so that Ireland can be virtually self-sufficient in wood at the turn of the century, a time of projected world shortage. Many forests are of single species, but where there is more variety and the location has scenic aspects, forest parks have been created throughout the country. One such park on the shores of a fishing lake, is Killykeen Forest ** near Cavan town which has an exquisite holiday home complex built completely from Irish timber.

The towns and villages of the Cooley peninsula have much to offer. Carlingford still has its medieval street pattern and a collection of interesting monuments in a good state of repair. The townspeople take good care of their village which contains a tholsel, a mint, Taaffe's Castle, an abbey and the imposing King John's Castle. The village of Greenore has a group of romantic English-style houses beside a lone group of Scots pine. They reflect a time when this port was owned by an English company. Whitestown is just what its name says: the whitewashed houses, some with a good thatch, often have their door and window details in light blue. The thatched roof is no longer seen as the poor man's solution, judging from the evidence of warm, honey-coloured roofs, sometimes stitched with patterns or shaved in different layers.

Journey to the Boyne Valley

Dundalk is a town with a hard-edge appearance. In some ways it is not unlike the nineteenth-century industrial towns of Northern Ireland. It is a town whose fortunes can vary with the fluctuations in taxes between Northern Ireland and the Republic. One pub-owner complained he had lost a lot of his Northern customers because of extra tax on drink. When, in my innocence, I asked why his former

** *See drawing on the title-page of this book.*

customers had no loyalty to their old pub he retorted: 'Loyalty, how are you. Mention the word loyalty to them Northerners and they think you are talking about the loyalists [unionists]. Besides, they are as tight [mean with money] as a crab's arse – and that's watertight!'

Heading south towards Ardee you pass a standing stone called Clochafarmore where the legendary Cúchulainn is supposed to have died. His commemorative statue in the General Post Office in Dublin shows him strapped to this pillar, so that even in death he could stand and face his enemies. Seeing the goddess of death, in the form of a black raven, land on his shoulder his enemies felt safe to approach. The choice of Cúchulainn's statue to commemorate the revolution of 1916 recognises the influence of the 'Celtic Twilight' on some of the leaders of that uprising. Interestingly, Ardee's Irish name means Ferdia's Ford, and recalls another key figure in the *Táin* epic. Cúchulainn and Ferdia were fostered together as children, but duty required them to fight for their respective provinces. Cúchulainn pleaded with Ferdia:

Small blessed virgin Mary sculpture on the wall of one of the 'Widows' houses' in Castlebellingham, near the main road to Dundalk

Detail of Muireadach's Cross, Monasterboice, probably depicting the arrest of Christ

Don't break our friendship and our bond,
don't break the oath we made once,
don't break our promise and our pledge.
Noble warrior, do not come.
After a bloody fight lasting days Cúchulainn gained a joyless victory:
Misery has befallen us,
Scáthacha's two foster-sons
– I, broken and blood red,
Your chariot standing empty.

Monasterboice

The monastic ruins of a round tower, three high crosses, early Christian grave slabs, a sundial and two churches can be found at Monasterboice. But what is really worth the effort of investigation is Muireadach's Cross. The monolithic cross is over five metres high and is the most beautiful high cross I have seen in Ireland. The detailed carved panels depict biblical scenes, such as the arrest and crucifixion of Christ, in an extended narrative form. This was a new departure from pagan Celtic art which had been essentially symbolic and ornamental. On Muireadach's Cross the ornament is mainly confined to the sides of the shaft and base. The top of the cross is crowned with a miniature church whose roof apex is similar to the full-size MacDara Church on the Galway island of the same name. The proportions, scale and detail of this cross are carefully balanced to give a whole that is greater than the sum of its parts. The depth of void enclosed by the circular ring linking the shaft and arms of the cross reminded me of some Henry Moore sculptures.

The journey from Monasterboice to the Boyne Valley passage graves passes Mellifont Abbey, the first Cistercian building in Ireland, and the pleasant village of Slane, where four matching Georgian houses face each other across the main crossroads. As in Westport county Mayo, the local lord was responsible for this formal arrangement. Lord Mount Charles has his Gothic revival castle nearby and his extensive grounds are sometimes used for rock concerts.

Boyne Valley

This valley contains three major passage-grave cemeteries at Knowth, Newgrange and Dowth. The first two are the most impressive, and Newgrange is the most accessible at present. Knowth may well become the most important when excavation is finally completed. The mound at Knowth is around twelve metres high and sixty-six metres wide and contains two passage graves between four and five thousand years old. There are many finely decorated kerb or base stones around the circumference of the mound. Some of these kerb stones were interfered with during the early Christian period when souterrains were dug into the base of the mound. Later still Gaelic kings had their residence there, before the Normans arrived and built a fort on top of the mound. A number of satellite tombs

surround the main mound in the shape of roundy hillocks or paps.

Beautifully maintained cottage near Castlebellingham. Note the shamrock roof-detail and the pleasant porch.

Newgrange

This mound is not as high as Knowth but is one-third wider. What is so special about this monument is its relationship to the winter solstice. Around 21 December the sun rises over a hill to the south – east of Newgrange at nine o'clock in the morning. The first shafts of sunlight penetrate through the 'window box' over the entrance to the passage. The golden light creeps up the upward sloping passage until it fully illuminates the large burial chamber for about seventeen minutes. Weather permitting, this event only occurs on a few days either side of the winter solstice. If you lie on the floor of the main burial chamber you will just see the window box. I cannot but marvel at the builders of this mound who were so accurate and precise that they could tell exactly the shortest day of the year. They also constructed the roof with drainage channels so that the chamber has remained dry for five thousand years. As always, the guides here are of a high standard and can answer any queries you may have.

Dowth

This unexcavated passage grave is bigger than Knowth but smaller than Newgrange. Access to the oldest chamber can be gained via a ladder through the top of the mound but you will have to crawl along the passage before reaching the burial chamber.

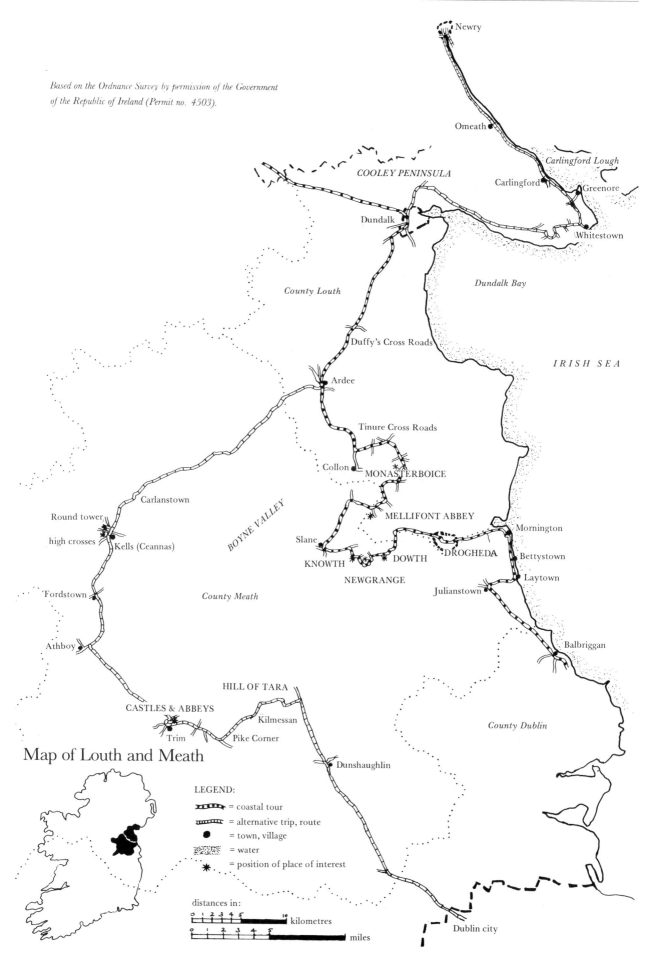

*Based on the Ordnance Survey by permission of the Government
of the Republic of Ireland (Permit no. 4503).*

Newry

Omeath

Carlingford Lough

COOLEY PENINSULA

Carlingford

Greenore

Dundalk

Whitestown

County Louth

Dundalk Bay

Duffy's Cross Roads

IRISH SEA

Ardee

Tinure Cross Roads

Collon

MONASTERBOICE

Carlanstown

BOYNE VALLEY

MELLIFONT ABBEY

Round tower

Mornington

high crosses

Slane

KNOWTH   DOWTH   **DROGHEDA**

Kells (Ceannas)

Bettystown

NEWGRANGE

Laytown

Fordstown

County Meath

Julianstown

Balbriggan

Athboy

HILL OF TARA

CASTLES & ABBEYS

Kilmessan

County Dublin

Trim   Pike Corner

Map of Louth and Meath

Dunshaughlin

LEGEND:

🚃🚃🚃 = coastal tour

🚃🚃🚃 = alternative trip, route

● = town, village

▨ = water

✳ = position of place of interest

distances in:

0 1 2 3 4 5   10 kilometres

0 1 2 3 4 5 miles

Dublin city

Alternative routes

Kells, Trim, Tara

At Ardee you might wish to divert to Kells, Trim and the Hill of Tara. The famous illuminated Book of Kells, now in Trinity College, Dublin came from the hands and minds of the monks who once lived here. There are high crosses, a round tower and a high-pitched oratory dedicated to the monastery's founder, St Columcille.

Trim has an extensive range of medieval buildings, the most striking of which is Trim Castle. Built in 1172 by the Normans, it is a massive ruin that still dominates the surrounding area. Strangely, it has a small golf course poking its way in and around the best Norman ruin in Ireland. This is because the castle and grounds are in the private ownership of Lord Dunsany who refuses to co-operate with those interested in this monument of great potential.

The Hill of Tara was the ancient palace of the high kings of Ireland. A series of earthworks remain, but nothing of the huge palace described in the old manuscripts. A place rich in history and mythology, but not in existing remains.

Coastal tour counties Louth and Meath

Route descriptions correspond with map on opposite page.

Route to Drogheda, Balbriggan
(Via N53 or R173) Dundalk – (N52) Duffy's Cross Roads – Ardee – (N2) direction Collon – (R169) – Tinure Cross Roads – Monasterboice – (R168) – Mellifont Abbey – (N2) Slane – (N51) – Knowth, Newgrange and Dowth – (N51) Drogheda – (All places of interest are signposted) (R150) Mornington – Bettystown – Laytown – Julianstown – (N1) Balbriggan (county Dublin).

Alternative routes

Carlingford or Cooley peninsula
Newry – (R173) Omeath – Carlingford – (R176) Greenore – Boharboy – Whitestown – (R173) – (N1) Dundalk.

Boyne Valley
Ardee – (N52) Carlanstown – Kells (Ceannanas): Round tower, high crosses – (R164) Fordstown – (N51) Athboy – (R154) Trim: castles and abbeys – (R154) Pike Corner – Kilmessan – Hill of Tara – (N3) Dunshaughlin – Dublin.

Trim Castle:
Not an epic, being not loosely architectured,
But with epic force, setting the head spinning
With the taut flight eastward of its bulk, King John's
Castle rams fast down the county of Meath.
This in its heavy ruin. New, a brute bright plateau,
It held speechless under its cold a whole province of Meath.
from 'King John's Castle' by Thomas Kinsella

The belfry of the ruined Howth Abbey
used to have three bells, which were rung
when someone died: one bell for a child,
two bells for a woman and three bells for
a man. The abbey dates from the twelfth
century.

Chapter 13

County Dublin

Most visitors to Ireland either arrive in, or depart from Dublin, yet many consider it not to be part of the 'real Ireland' which they have travelled far to explore. This attitude may be partly explained by the 'green' packaging of Ireland by its own tourist board abroad. Dublin may appear a shabby capital in comparison to better-known European cities, but that is only a half truth which ignores its superior physical setting beside the sea within easy reach of beaches and mountains. If possible you should try to visit the beautiful peninsula of Howth and the picturesque Dalkey area. Howth in particular retains a strong village identity because of its connection with the large local fishing fleet. Howth head also offers fine cliff walks and views over Dublin bay.

Perhaps the clearly visible poverty of beggars and ghetto housing districts, plus the attendant theft and drug problems, new to Ireland but a familiar story to many visitors, encourage a quick departure from Dublin to the 'real Ireland' of green and legend. However, the greater Dublin area contains one in three of the Republic of Ireland's population and that fact alone should make its Irishness real enough.

But most of all Dublin is a state of mind as well as a place. You need to get 'under the skin' of Dublin and its citizens as well as eying the shops and monuments. A few days' stay is worth while, because it gives you an insight into modern Irish society and takes away the common misunderstanding that this country is twenty years behind the rest of Europe. Ireland is poorer than many other western European countries, but when the comparison is widened its relative position improves, and it is well within the top twenty-five per cent of the countries of the world in terms of wealth.

I don't want to reproduce what the tourist office brochures say about Dublin. The _Tourist Trail_ and _The Dublin Guide_ brochures provide lots of information to accompany their signposted walking tour of Dublin with all the relevant information about who built what, lived where and died when. I'll give my favourite places along with my observations of its people and history.

Your first day in Dublin is always your worst.
from _The Dream Songs_ 299 by John Berryman

Brief history

The first international noting of Dublin was by the Greek geographer Ptolemy in AD 140, who called it Eblana, now the name of a Dublin theatre. When the Vikings arrived in 840 they established themselves on a section of ground between the river Liffey and Christ Church Cathedral known as the 'dark pool' or _Dubhlinn_ in Irish, from which the name Dublin derives. However, Irish purists nowadays prefer the older Irish name _Baile Átha Cliath,_ because it refers to a river crossing, near the present Heuston Station, made before the Vikings arrived.

The Vikings brought city living to Ireland and developed many east coast towns, but Dublin remained their capital. For two

This was never my town
I was not born nor bred
Nor schooled here and she will not
Have me alive or dead
But yet she holds my mind with her seedy
elegance.
from 'Dublin' by Louis MacNeice

centuries they held Dublin until they and their Irish allies were defeated at Clontarf, now a north Dublin suburb, by the high king of Ireland. In 1171 the Normans fought their way north from Wexford to capture Dublin. It was not to be until 1922 that the local population gained control again.

In the intervening centuries Dublin was to become the centre of English power in Ireland. For a brief period in the late eighteenth century Dublin had a functioning parliament under the overall control of London. Many, if not most, of Dublin's old public buildings date from that period of urban expansion. Fearing that Ireland might slip out of its controlling grasp, and worried by the 1798 revolt by the United Irishmen calling for a republic, the English parliament resumed complete direct control of Irish affairs. The city of Dublin suffered the loss of a resident ruling class. For the same reason, the full force of the industrial revolution never struck Dublin and its size increased slowly until the 1950s, when it began to explode in size. Within thirty-five years the population of Greater Dublin doubled, as Ireland experienced a shift in population from rural to urban areas along with a dramatic increase in population as emigration, which had been very common, slowed down. This rapid urbanisation has caused huge suburbs and resulted in the swallowing up of surrounding towns and villages such as Malahide, Swords, Dalkey and Lucan.

The very young average age of the Irish population means that Ireland has a very high dependency ratio, with each person at work

supporting two people. This proportion is almost double that of most EEC countries. As a result, the Irish income per person is approximately sixty per cent that of Britain and fifty per cent that of Denmark, Holland and West Germany. In short, Ireland has a young and growing population but has not got as much money as it needs to provide the same services as advanced western European countries. Like other developed countries, poverty is now largely urban-based in Ireland, and particularly Dublin-based.

There has been a significant rise in urban crime, such as house burglary, car theft and handbag-snatching in the Dublin area. However, Ireland as a whole has a crime level of about two-thirds that of Holland, Denmark, Italy, Britain, or France. There is no reason to be paranoid about crime, but you should take sensible precautions when staying in Dublin, as you would in any other large city.

Dublin's fair city

'In Dublin's fair city where the girls are so pretty' goes a popular old ballad which is sometimes sung at football matches. I'll come to 'the girls' later, but first the 'fair city'. Dublin had a pleasant, low-rise and predominantly eighteenth- and early nineteenth-century city centre until it was transformed by a rash of new commercial and office developments begun in the 1960s. Whole areas of the city

A very elaborate entrance to a house on the hill of Howth. The entrances to houses in general in Ireland are very important and often emphasised by porches, gates or hedges. The rear of houses is treated with less care, if not completely neglected, as can be seen when you travel by DART-train in Dublin.

If you drive from Howth to Malahide, you will have this view of the estuary near Portmarnock

Howth-fish-smokery

A fish smokery in Howth harbour. Unfortunately the coherence of the older buildings on the quay has been ruined by a new, very ugly iceplant.

centre have been depopulated and replaced by crude office blocks. Some of these areas have not been redeveloped and now lie derelict, or are used as temporary car parks. The 'fair city' has taken a beating and has emerged battered, cynical, but not totally defeated.

Public opinion has become more aware of what makes a living city, but whether that awareness will influence future city development remains to be seen. Destructive road-widening, which has gutted Belfast and countless other cities such as Brussels, is still planned for Dublin. Uncoordinated and monofunctional plans, rather than integrated urban design, are knocking the teeth out of a once-smiling city centre. Some of the worst offenders are the pension fund insurance corporations who invest Dubliners' money to destroy Dublin with ugly shopping centres and dreary and scaleless office blocks. The City Corporation of Dublin has not given good example either with their bunker-like civic offices on the valuable archaeological site of Wood Quay where the Vikings first settled. The citizens objected to the building of these offices and the destruction of the site and there were protest marches of half a million people, but to no avail. Bureaucracy in Ireland, and in Dublin in particular, tends to be monolithic, secretive, unprofessional, uncoordinated and not very democratic. Dubliners have watched their city change for the worse with a stoic resignation and an occasional outburst of frustration.

The city centre is compact compared to Dublin's overall size and it is relatively easy to orientate yourself. O'Connell Street is the city's main street but its potential is diminished by shoddy hamburger places and lots of litter. The GPO or General Post Office is a national shrine because the headquarters of the 1916 revolution* was located here. Public meetings are often addressed from under the portico or from the back of a lorry parked before the Ionic columns. The same portico shelters revolutionary newspaper-sellers on Saturdays and in the summer groups of French and Spanish students over here to learn English – whenever they are not talking in their own language. At the St Patrick's Day parade in March the official rostrum is located opposite this portico so as to give a good view to the enclosed VIPs of the goose-fleshed, high-stepping American school bands. Close by is the monument to the trade unionist James Larkin, who led a strike in 1913 to which the employers responded with a famous lock-out. A man who thrived on the heroic, he would have been amused with the young child, obviously a television watcher, who asked his father about the green statue 'Hey da, is that the incredible hulk?' Henry Street, the pedestrian street next to the GPO, is the busiest shopping street in Dublin and items are generally cheaper here than in the more upmarket Grafton Street area. Moore Street harbours the hallowed institution of Dublin street-traders and metric measurement has yet to gain a toe-hold here. Sturdy ladies wrapped in warm woolly coats and leather boots stand on upturned crates beside their prams and bawl in Dublinese 'Ten for eighty pence the apples!' Unless you are a regular customer you may get stuck with some bashed apples at the bottom of the bag, although the price is usually low. I've seen some beggars being given fruit at the end of the day by these hardy but not heartless ladies. A huge amount of rubbish accumulates by evening time. The single most objectionable habit I have seen in Ireland is the careless and casual throwing around of litter and rubbish wherever groups of people go.

The shopping centre adjoining Henry Street and Moore Street is called the ILAC (Irish Life Assurance Company) Centre, although I've heard it called the 'Lilac Centre' by some Dubliners. Maybe the additional L stands for lousy or lamentable but certainly not for lovely or likeable.

This is not a strike, it is a lock-out of the men who have been tyrannically treated by a most unscrupulous scoundrel...
By the living God, if they want war, they can have it.
James Larkin, 26 August 1913

On the north side of Howth lies Bailey light-house

St Michan's Church: history rewritten

This is an old church much renovated in the nineteenth century but without any great architectural attributes. What makes it interesting is the vaults which preserve from decay the interred dead bodies, some of which are hundreds of years old. St Michan's may have inspired Dubliner Bram Stoker to write his first Dracula story, but it was the scene of rewritten history some years ago. A friend of mine and some of his pals were dodging school and went to Michan's to pass the time and 'shake the hand of the crusader'. While in the vault with the tour group my friend and his pals got bored and started 'messing around' until he fell on one of the bodies and punctured its chest. The inflamed guide pulled him by the ear and threw him out after taking his name and address. Some fifteen years later my friend was asked by visiting workmates from London to bring them to Michan's vault. Although nervous and reluctant at first, he thought that he was sufficiently disguised from his wayward school days, with a new droopy moustache and long curly hair, as to be unrecognisable. Besides, the old guide must surely have retired or even been interred in the vaults himself. Fortified with such self-assurances and a pint of stout, he brought his two friends to the gate lodge of the church. He felt weak at the knees and dry in the mouth when he spotted the same old guide call the waiting tour to order. Time had worn the old man, but he still seemed capable of pulling an ear and his filmy eyes did seem to linger on his moustache. Schoolboy intuition told my friend to stay at the back of the group as everyone filed down the steps to the cobwebbed vaults. A terrible feeling of *déjà vu* overtook him and sweat beaded his forehead. Horror beyond a Dracula kiss seized him when an 'old bat [eccentric woman] of a tourist' asked, 'How come this body has a hole in the chest?' My friend's long legs could have taken him up the cellar steps before his ear was pulled again but he still would have to face his London workmates; so he stayed still and promised God he would give up drink and women if he escaped this ordeal. And escape he did. Without batting his filmy eyes, the old guide answered authoritatively 'That's where he was run through with a sword, madam', and continued on with his well-learnt patter.

The Quays, Ryan's pub and 'the Park'

Close to Michan's is the green dome of the Four Courts. You can look inside the fine circular waiting hall under that beautiful dome that allows light through its apex. If it's around ten in the morning you may see all the barristers, resplendent in their gowns and wigs, chatting to their clients. The air reverberates with their talk as if the dome was full of swarming bees. Don't try to take photographs or you may see more of the building than you reckoned.

The quays of Dublin were once full of antique shops, second-hand book stores, pubs and houses. Road-widening plans have blighted the area, but some antique shops remain. Some may be closer to junk than antiques, but if you like rummaging there is no better place.

The Casino, Marino, on the north side of Dublin city, off the Malahide Road. It is an eighteenth-century miniature classical temple of three storeys, but on the outside it appears to be only one, because the basement is below ground level, while ground and first floor are not distinguished in the facade. The plan is based on a Greek cross and the very interesting building is amazingly spacious inside, with many very unusual features, of which the most ingenious is the door in the hall of the ground floor, which can be replaced by a sliding down window! The splendidly inlaid timber floors, plaster ceilings and silk wallpaper of this national monument have been painstakingly restored by the Office of Public Works and the tour led by one of their guides is very informative.

Ryan's pub in Parkgate Street is worthy of diversion for its own sake or as a stopping post on route to the huge Phoenix Park. It is a beautifully designed pub with every corner crafted with care and attention to detail. Access to the snugs (enclosed spaces within a pub) is an unusual privilege. The barman pulls a chain which allows the door to open and once inside no one can come in, unless the lock is released from the inside. Fine 'whiskey' mirrors give a spacious airy feeling to the small spaces which are lovely and bright with daylight spilling in from the rear rooflight. At night soft yellow light twinkles on the old brass work which cleaners' 'elbow grease' keeps sparkling.

The Phoenix Park is a great amenity for western Dublin and consists of 740 hectares of sports fields, woodland, small pools, a people's park and Dublin Zoo, which is pleasantly laid out along a small lake and is a great place to bring children bored with travel. As well as Gaelic and soccer football grounds there is a cricket club and a polo ground, reminders of adopted colonial games. Cricket seems so inactive except for the batsman and bowler, compared to the jostling on the polo pitch. The elaborate horse boxes and Mercedes speak of an affluence not many Dubliners enjoy. The president of Ireland and the American ambassador's residence occupy former colonial government houses and large sections of parkland. One thing you should notice are the well-designed gas lamps dating from 1860 found throughout 'the Park' as most Dubliners call it.

The Liberties

If you cross the river near Heuston Station and climb Stevens Lane you will meet James's Street and Guinness's brewery, where for the trouble of watching a video about the famous black beer you can enjoy free a cool creamy half-pint of stout. Nearby is the Guinness Hop Store, well renovated and used now for exhibitions. The surrounding area is called the Liberties, a virtually self-sufficient part of the city with its own shops, street-traders and markets. This area once stood outside the jurisdiction of the medieval town, which is how it got its name. The Liberties has suffered population displacement to the suburbs, but still retains its identity.

Three-storey shops with offices and flats on Thomas Street give way to two-storey houses on Meath Place and finally to single-storey cottages in enclosed courtyards such as Brabazon Square. Blocks of flats built in the early 1960s ignored existing street patterns and were out of scale with their older neighbours, but happily more recent housing is sympathetic in location and scale.

The National College of Art and Design is situated in an old whiskey distillery in Thomas Street where the students add an extra burst of colour to the local scene. I heard one unflappable street-trader comment to another after serving a girl student dressed in seductive black bandages 'That's a right quare get-up your wan [that woman] has on her. I wonder how the young fellas [boys] can study, with her parading around?' The other trader answered 'Would ye go on out of that, sure I heard tell that they have naked models over there for all to draw and sure she [the student] is covered where it counts.'

When money's tight and is hard to get
And your horse also ran,
When all you have is a heap of debt
A PINT OF PLAIN IS YOUR ONLY MAN.
from *At Swim-Two-Birds* by Flann O'Brien

In the Liberties many older women go out shopping very early in the morning

Kids eating crisps

Two cathedrals

Christ Church and St Patrick's are cathedrals dating from the eleventh and twelfth centuries respectively. St Patrick's was built by a Norman baron/bishop in an attempt to supersede Christ Church as the principal place of worship in Dublin. St Patrick's is my favourite mainly because of its choir. Try and plan your visit to coincide with choir recitals or practice. Choir-boys in long red cassocks with stiff white collars walk in ceremonial procession under the fading banners of old heroes and soldiers. Even Jonathan Swift, author of *Gulliver's Travels* and Dean of St Patrick's, must startle in his cathedral tomb when he hears the boys' voices soar to the roofbeams. One choir-boy I met waiting for practice to begin showed me around the sights of the cathedral. I asked him did he like singing with the famous choir, but he gave me that common Irish answer couched in negative rather than positive terminology: 'It's not too bad, it could be worse.' And I used to think protestants had a work ethic!

'The Green' and Grafton Street

St Stephen's Green, known affectionately as 'the Green' was once an ancient commonage and was laid out in its present design in the 1880s with money from the Guinness family. It is a fine mixture of formal and romantic landscape design that manages to give the impression of being larger than it actually is. Merrion Square not far away only capitalises on fifty per cent of its potential because it fails to create focal points, exploit views or have a design philosophy. In either of these parks on a summer day with only a glimmer of sunshine you will see 'the girls' in filmsy cotton dresses pulled above their knees, absorbing every golden ray of the sun. In quiet and not-so-quiet corners of the park there is widespread hugging and cuddling which you would not see in more 'liberal' European countries. Maybe it's because these young adults have no place of their own to share private feelings, since many of them live at home until they marry.

Grafton Street is where the youth of Dublin fashion parade. Friends from home have commented on how up to date youth fashion is in Ireland. Why they thought it should be otherwise says something about their preconceived ideas about 'romantic Ireland'. Yet there is a tyranny of fashion in Dublin. Three basic styles can be noticed, the trendy and *haute couture* dressers, the remnants of the jeans brigade and the alternative dressers. But if you don't fit neatly into a category you are stared at in a very obvious way. This Irish habit of staring takes time to get used to, but it is more related to idle curiosity than ignorant behaviour.

Grafton Street is full of sandwich-board and placard-holding men in poor circumstances, whose signs ask you to eat here or have your hair cut there. A Dublin institution by the name of Bewley's is a coffee, tea and bakery shop in Grafton Street, although I prefer their other shop in Westmoreland Street. During my first weeks in Dublin I was puzzled by men in Grafton Street shouting 'pepe' and 'Herl-r-Pres' only to discover they meant 'papers' and 'Herald or Press' (the Dublin evening papers).

An accordion-player busking in Grafton Street

Trinity College, Dublin centre: view of the cobbled Front (or Parliament) Square and two of the youngest buildings, the 1937 Reading Room and the 1978 Arts Block

College Green and traffic

Crossing the road near Trinity College the way Dubliners do it is amazing. Everyone dodges their way through the cars, until forced to give way by the 'double decker' buses, who are the kings and bullies of city traffic. A drive around town in the front seat on the upper deck is a must for every visitor. There's nothing better to get your adrenalin going as the driver lurches and darts through the heavy traffic. The last bus home at night sees these huge buses career along like juggernauts, screeching to a squeaky halt whenever someone manages to ring the stop bell. One man's false teeth flew two seats and landed in my neighbour's lap when the driver suddenly slammed on the brakes to avoid an unlit cyclist. The gummy owner of the teeth, who was more than a little merry, shouted to the driver, as he rolled up his sleeves 'Come back here you bowsy [rascal] and I'll knock out your shaggin' teeth.' The laughter of the passengers and the return of his teeth dissolved the man's anger. Remember that a bus with _An Lár_ on it is going – or is supposed to be going – to the city centre.

Trinity College is an oasis in the middle of a busy city. Laid out in a succession of squares it is a nice place to wander around, whether you visit the beautiful Book of Kells housed here or not. Founded in 1591, it contains a fine collection of buildings from the eighteenth to the twentieth century. Lunchtime concerts and plays are worth watching out for. Oliver Goldsmith and Samuel Beckett were students here.

A conversation overheard between a passenger and a bus conductor. Passenger: Holy hour, have the bus fares gone up again? Conductor: Do you work or are you a full-time actor?

Museums

Like any capital Dublin has a good collection of museums and art galleries. My favourite is the National Museum in Kildare Street, with its collection of early Irish treasures. Some displays could be better but it is a pleasant building with lots to see. Next door is the parliament building.

The Chester Beatty Library at 20 Shrewsbury Road has a very special collection of ancient Babylonian clay tablets, exquisite oriental manuscripts, albums, picture scrolls and Greek and Egyptian papyri. If you like oriental and arabic art then this museum is a must for you.

Georgian Dublin

The first terrace of Georgian houses was built in Henrietta Street near the Kings Inns. Much of the old north city was Georgian and very fashionable until bankruptcy affected some of its landlords and the buildings became the tenements so well described in James Plunkett's *Strumpet City*. Areas such as Gardiner Street have been rebuilt with new housing, which is fine in itself but lacks the necessary scale the taller Georgian houses had to create an urban feeling. The area from Merrion Square to Fitzwilliam Square, south of the river, probably has the best collection of Georgian houses, laid out in squares and avenues as they were intended to be seen. The carefully ordered and austere facades hide spacious rooms with fine plasterwork. Hume Street and St Stephen's Green East have office blocks with fake Georgian facades, even false front doors set against concrete walls.

Watch out too for the coal holes set in the pavement, some have very good designs. It is a pity the lovely granite paving slabs have been replaced by dull and slippery concrete throughout old Dublin. Granite kerbs have survived municipal vandalism but only in places near Trinity College and the Bank of Ireland are the original granite slabs remaining.

Sports

A visit to Croke Park to see a Gaelic football or hurling match on a Sunday afternoon can be very enjoyable. Provincial finals and all-Ireland finals are played throughout July, August and September. Gaelic games are fast and physical, but neither players nor officials get paid as soccer players do. The game of hurling is particularly skilful and remarkably fast-moving, although Gaelic football has the largest following. You need not worry either about crowd hooliganism – it is virtually unknown at Gaelic games.

Horse-racing is available at the Phoenix Park and Leopardstown race courses. I like the Phoenix Park course where all social groups seem to meet to study 'the form', watch the fashionable ladies, place bets and have a few drinks. The serious punters have dozens of race-meeting tags hanging from their binoculars. The women have pillbox hats and the men jaunty felt ones, while the jockeys doff their riding hats when they meet the horse-owner in the paddock. Horse breeding and training is a big industry in Ireland. Betting is easy and you might be lucky like me and win on your first race.

This former Martello tower in Sandycove now houses the James Joyce Museum. Sandycove was the setting for the opening of *Ulysses:* Stately, plump Buck Mulligan blessed Dublin Bay from its gunrest while Stephen Dedalus surveyed 'the scrotumtightening sea'. Martello towers were erected on the Irish east coast around the early 1800s for protection against a Napoleonic invasion.

Based on the Ordnance Survey by permission of the Government of the Republic of Ireland (Permit no. 4503).

Playing with words

Ireland is one of the top book buying countries in the world and
municipal libraries are well used. Your average Dubliner is not
particularly dedicated to literature, although she or he can throw a
quote of some literary master, when you are least expecting it. What
Dubliners and their country cousins love is the playing with words,
when the 'crack' flows at parties and pubs.

    G.B. Shaw disliked the city and preferred Dalkey before he moved
to London. He saw 'no seed of culture' when he left, although the
literary revival of the Celtic Twilight** caused him to reconsider that

** *See page 121*

Joxer's song, Joxer's song – give us wan of your shut-eyed wans.
from *Juno and the Paycock* by Seán O'Casey

It's only a little cold I have; there's nothing derogatory wrong with me.
from *The Plough and the Stars* by Seán O'Casey

Into his mind came that other book *Portrait of the Artist*. Here had been renunciation of family, faith, even birthland and the promise of silence, exile and cunning. What dit there seem to be here? The garrulous, the repatriate, the ingenious.
from *The Dalkey Archive* by Flann O'Brien.

A humble Jesuit would be like a dog without a tail or a woman without a knickers on her.
from *The Hard Life* by Flann O'Brien

comment. W.B. Yeats, a Dubliner by birth but a Sligoman by desire, found his niche in the Abbey Theatre and public acclaim. James Joyce, like many Dubliners, was a little cool towards the misty Celtic Twilight of Yeats and somewhat sour towards his native city which he left in 1904. He once wrote that while Dublin 'had been a capital for thousands of years' no artist 'had given it to the world.' His books *Dubliners* and *Ulysses* did just that. Joyce had lived in more than twenty different houses, because of his father's gradually declining financial situation, and included many of them in *Ulysses*. The book gives a meticulous record of Dublin's buildings, pubs and brothels, many of which now have disappeared.

Sean O'Casey, labour activist and writer, caught the Irish mood at the dawn of independence with plays like *Shadow of a Gunman* and *Juno and the Paycock*. My 'Irish grandmother' shared a house with O'Casey on the North Circular Road during that period and reckons she can recognise a number of her friends in his plays. She once asked him where he got the conversation for Dublin characters, like Joxer Daly. Sean squinted his poor eyes and said; 'Sure, I sit in a snug*** and listen to the men talking and drinking outside.' But the 'boorzwawze' [bourgeoisie] turned on him with his play *The Plough and the Stars*, and he too left Ireland.

From the late 1930s until the early 1960s Flann O'Brien was to capture the absurd wit and whimsy of Dubliners in his books and newspaper articles. Characters such as 'the brother' have passed into the vernacular of pub chat. He relates hilarious cattle raids along the North Circular Road in his book *At Swim-Two-Birds*. Joyce would have approved.

Brendan Behan captured an international audience in the late 1950s as much by his behaviour as by his plays. His short life is remembered fondly by many Dubliners although, like many Irishmen, he found greater acclaim in death than in life.

Some of the forementioned plays are performed regularly in Dublin's theatres, so if you come across an announcement for one of them, do go along! Irish theatre in general is of good quality, fully alive and well attended too. I saw the performance of Hugh Leonard's *Da*, about a Dublin father-son relationship, in the pleasant Abbey Theatre. I found it funny, perceptive and touching.

All these plays and books recall an earlier twentieth-century Dublin, much of which has disappeared. Some would say that parts of it were falling down, before property dealers knocked it down for lucrative and sterile office blocks. Physically Dublin city could become as characterless as, for instance, Rotterdam in the Netherlands, if it continues this way without vision or municipal initiative. Rotterdam had no choice when the bombs fell during the war, but Dublin can learn from past mistakes.

Dublin is more than this or that place or writer. It doesn't stand still in a loop of time, awaiting the momentary thud of the developers' wrecking ball or the immortality of *Ulysses*. Moaning and groaning mixes with warmth and repartee. Winters can be sooty, dark and damp, but Christmas and New Year are never dull, with your glass always full. Summer skies can be folded into cloudy darkness, but the cloudscapes are always imposing and the frequent rainbows an artist's delight.

*** See page 171

It is summer in Ireland now and our journey is over. Soft rain gives way to bright light on the lush green of blooming Howth. The bay is filling in the evening sun under the pull of a new moon and the plough in the stars will twinkle tonight. City children leave the beach with their buckets, but one left me her logic: 'You know what? The sun and moon keep moving because they cannot find a soft seat.'

Coastal tour county Dublin

Route descriptions correspond with map on opposite page.

Route to Howth Head and Dalkey
Julianstown (N1) – Balbriggan – (R127) Skerries – (R128) Rush – Lusk: Round Tower – (R127) – (N1) Swords – (R106) Malahide – Portmarnock – Sutton – Howth: St Mary's Abbey – Clontarf – Dublin centre – Blackrock – Dún Laoghaire – Dalkey: island/church.

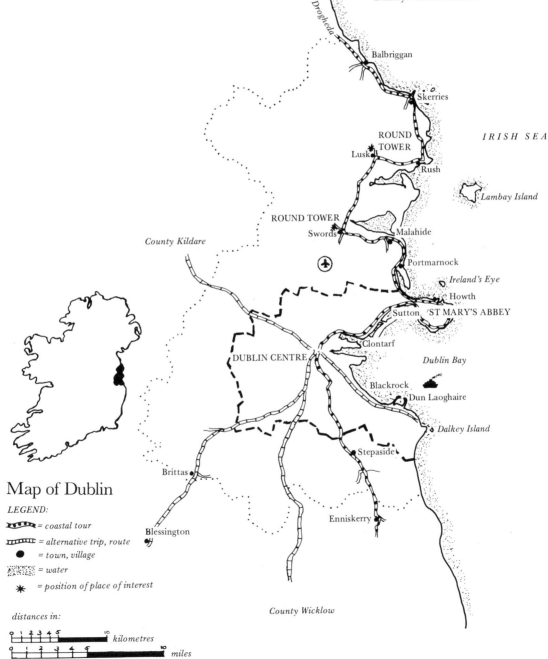

Map of Dublin

LEGEND:

- = coastal tour
- = alternative trip, route
- = town, village
- = water
- = position of place of interest

distances in:

kilometres

miles

Based on the Ordnance Survey by permission of the Government of the Republic of Ireland (Permit no. 4503).

Index

A

B

C

Bibliography

Böll, Heinrich. *Irish Journal: A Traveller's Portrait of Ireland.* London: Secker and Warburg, 1983.

Clarke, Austin. *Poems 1917-1938.* Dublin: Dolmen Press, 1974.

Cunningham, George. *Burren Journey.* Limerick, Ireland: Shannonside Mid Western Regional Tourism Organisation, 1978.

Curriculum Development Unit. *The Celtic Way of Life.* Dublin: O'Brien Educational, 1976.

_____ *A World of Stone: The Aran Islands.* Dublin: O'Brien Educational, 1977.

Curtis, Edmund. *A History of Ireland.* London: Methuen, 1961.

Egan, Thomas A. *Ballintubber Abbey.* Mayo, Ireland: By the Author, Ballintubber Abbey, 1967.

Facts about Ireland. Dublin: Department of Foreign Affairs, 1978.

Flower, Robin: *The Irish Tradition.* London: Oxford University Press, 1947.

Gmelch, Sharon. *Tinkers and Travellers.* Dublin: O'Brien Press, 1979.

Guinness, Desmond, and Ryan, William. *Irish Houses and Castles. London: Thames and Hudson, 1971.*

Harbison, Peter. Guide to the National Monuments in the Republic of Ireland. Dublin: Gill and Macmillan, 1970.

Heaney, Seamus. *Door Into the Dark.* London: Faber and Faber, 1969.

_____ *Field Work.* London: Faber and Faber, 1979.

_____ *North.* London: Faber and Faber, 1975.

Ireland Guide. Dublin: Irish Tourist Board - Bord Failte, 1982.

Kinsella, Thomas. *Selected Poems 1956-1968.* Dublin: Dolmen Press, 1973.

_____ trans. *The Tain.* London: Oxford University Press, 1970.

Lavin, Mary. *Happiness and Other Stories.* London: Constable, 1969.

Leask, Harold. *St. Patrick's Rock Cashel.* Dublin: Stationery Office.

MacCana, Proinsias. *Celtic Mythology.* Middlesex, England: Newnes Books, 1983.

MacCurtain, Margaret., gen. ed. *A History of Ireland.* Dublin: Gill and Macmillan, 1969. *The Birth of Modern Ireland, by Mark Tierney and Margaret MacCurtain.*

_____ gen. ed. *A History of Ireland.* Dublin: Gill and Macmillan, 1969. *Conquests and Colonisation,* by M.E. Collins.

McGahern, John. *Getting Through.* London: Quartet Books, 1979.

_____ *The Leavetaking.* London: Quartet Books, 1977.

MacLoughlin, Adrian. *Streets of Ireland.* Dublin: Swift Publications, 1981.

McMahon, Seán., ed. *A Book of Irish Quotations.* Dublin: O'Brien Press, 1984.

McNally, Kenneth. *The Islands of Ireland.* London: Batsford, 1978.

Meyer, Kuno., trans. *Selections from Ancient Irish Poetry.* London: Constable, 1959.

O'Brien, Edna. *The Country Girls.* Harmondsworth, England: Penguin, 1980.

_____ *The Girl With Green Eyes.* Harmondsworth, England: Penguin, 1980.

_____ *A Pagan Place.* Harmondsworth, England: Penguin, 1971.

O'Brien, Kate. *Without My Cloak.* Harmondsworth, England: Penguin, 1949.

O'Casey, Sean. *Autobiographies 1.* London: Macmillan, 1963.

O'Conchuir, Doncha. *Treoir Guide: Corca Dhuibhne its Peoples and their Buildings.* Translated by Bryan MacMahon, Tralee, Ireland: Cló Dhuibhne, 1977.

O'Connor, Frank. *The Little Monasteries.* Dublin: Dolmen Press, 1976.

O'Criomhthain, Thomas. *The Islanders.* London: Oxford University Press, 1978.

O'hAodha, Michael. *The O'Casey Enigma.* Dublin: Mercier Press, 1980.

O'Meara, John., trans. *The Voyage of Saint Brendan.* Dublin: Dolmen Press, 1978.

One Hundred Best Irish Songs and Ballads. Dublin: Mac Publications, n.d.

Ordnance Survey Road Atlas of Ireland. London: Macmillan, 1985.

Ó Ríordáin, Seán P. *Antiquities of the Irish Countryside.* London: Methuen, 1965.

O'Shea, Tim. *The Skelligs.* Cahirciveen, Ireland: By the Author, 1985.

O'Sullivan, Maurice. *Twenty Years A-Growing.* London: Oxford University Press, 1983.

O'Tuama, Sean., ed. *An Duanaire 1600-1900: Poems of the Dispossessed.* Dublin: Dolmen Press, 1981.

Plunkett, James. *Strumpet City.* London: Arrow, 1978.

Powell, T.G.E. *The Celts.* London: Thames and Hudson, 1980.

Rees, Alwyn., and Rees, Brinley. *Celtic Heritage.* London: Thames and Hudson, 1961.

Ryan, John. *Clonmacnois: A Historical Summary.* Dublin: Stationery Office, 1973.

Sayers, Peig. *An Old Woman's Reflections.* London: Oxford University Press, 1978.

Severin, Tim. *The Brendan Voyage.* London: Arena, 1983.
Sharkey, John. *Celtic Mysteries.* London: Thames and Hudson, 1975.
Synge, John Millington. *Collected Works.* Vol. 2: *Prose.* London: Oxford University Press, 1966.

Acknowledgements

Quotations in this book are taken from the following publications: *His Toy, His Dream, His Rest* by John Berryman (Faber); *Poems 1917-1938* by Austin Clarke (Dolmen 1974); *The Irish Tradition* by Robin Flower (Oxford 1947); *Translations* by Brian Friel (Faber 1980); *Door Into The Dark* by Seamus Heaney (Faber 1969); *Field Work* by Seamus Heaney (Faber 1979); *North* by Seamus Heaney (Faber 1975); *The Selected John Hewitt* by John Hewitt (Blackstaff Press); *The Penguin Book of Irish Verse* by Brendan Kennelly (Penguin); *Selected Poems 1956-1968* by Thomas Kinsella (Dolmen 1973); *The Tain* by Thomas Kinsella (Oxford 1970); '*Letter to Derek Mahon*' by Michael Longley (Northern Ireland Arts Council); *The Collected Poems of Louis MacNeice* by Louis MacNeice (Faber); *The Faber Book of Irish Verse* by John Montague (Faber); *A Grafted Tongue* by John Montague (Dolmen); *At Swim-Two Birds* by Flann O'Brien (Grafton); *The Dalkey Archive* by Flann O'Brien (Grafton); *The Hard Life* by Flann O'Brien (Grafton); *Juno and the Paycock* by Sean O'Casey (Macmillan); *The Plough and the Stars* by Sean O'Casey (Macmillan); *The Big Fellow* by Frank O'Connor (A.D. Peters); *The Islandman* by Thomas Ó Criomhthainn (Oxford); *The Short Stories of Liam O'Flaherty* (A.D. Peters); *One Hundred Best Irish Songs and Ballads* by Mac Publications; *An Duanaire 1600-1900: Poems of the Dispossessed* by Sean O'Tuama and Thomas Kinsella (Dolmen 1981); *The Collected Poems of W.B. Yeats* (Macmillan, Michael B. Yeats, A.P. Watt Ltd).

If any breach of copyright has been inadvertently committed the publishers apologise; copyright holders are invited to contact the publishers and any such breach will be rectified in subsequent editions.

A Word of Thanks

It has taken over two years for *Ireland explored* to grow from a very challenging idea to complete publication. From the time I fell in love with an Irishman, I also became very interested in Ireland, about which I knew very little at first. This interest resulted in another 'big love' for her physical beauty, rich culture and moving history, which has been the source of inspiration for making this book.

I have received a great deal of encouragement and help from people, both in Ireland and in the Netherlands, during the completion of this travel diary. Among these were the helpful staff of the Department of Visual Communications of the National College of Art and Design, and in particular the head of the department, Bill Bolger; I would like to thank Joe Little of Radio Telefis Eireann for organising viewings of many file-films on Ireland in the RTE library; Seán Andrews, who patiently read and corrected my material and suggested improvements; Gerard O'Sullivan, who helped me to complete the elaborate tour maps; my special friend from Holland, who is fond of red wine, cigars and masterpieces; Bert Zeijlstra, all-round book designer, for his advice and knowledge of wine and ten-year-old brandy; and Majo Joostens, for her excellent assistance with the paste-up.

'Ireland explored' is not just a catchy title, for the testing of possible suitable places of interest or beauty took more than 12.000 kilometres of travilling. My husband, Ciarán O'Connor, has been very involved in this project from the very start, spent all his holidays of the last two years joining me on my tours and took the result, a rapidly ageing new car, for granted! His wide knowledge of his native country was constantly at my disposal and this book could not have been completed without his continuous stimulation, encouragement and invaluable assistance.

About the author

Ditty Kummer was born in the Netherlands and qualified as a graphic designer from the Arnhem Academy of Visual Arts in 1976. After her studies she worked free-lance as a graphic designer, as a teacher in the Arnhem Academy of Architecture, and as an editor of a monthly magazine until 1983. During her holidays she produced many private travel diaries and illustrated stories, which eventually resulted in a wish to compile a complete travel guide on Ireland. Through a post-graduate year of studies at the National College of Art and Design in Dublin, she began the explore her subject, the result of which is this book.

She now lives permanently in Dublin and teaches in the Department of Architecture at the Dublin Institute of Technology.